More 1   *h*

A New Vocabulary

C. W. E. Kirk-Greene

PACKARD PUBLISHING LIMITED

CHICHESTER

More Fluent French

A New Vocabulary

© 2008 C. W. E. Kirk-Greene

Reprinted with additions and amendments 2010

First published by Packard Publishing Limited, Forum house, Stirling Road, Chichester, West Sussex, PO19 7DN, UK.

ISBN 978 185341 140 3 paperback

A CIP catalogue record of this book is available from the British Library.

The cover photograph is of the Hôtel de Ville and War Memorial, La Haye-Pesnel, Normandy, 2008.

Prepared for press by Michael Packard.
Laid out by Hilite Design & Reprographics Limited, Southampton, Hampshire.
Printed and bound in the United Kingdom by DPS Partnership Limited, Burgess Hill, West Sussex.

Preface

My sources for this book have been various, but my reading of French newspapers has been especially valuable. The topics reported in the French press are often the same as those appearing in Britain, so it is interesting to see the vocabulary used. Thus part of the book deals with topical words that reflect the times we live in. There is the perennial but stimulating challenge for all linguists of trying to keep up to date. It must be emphasized here that I do not necessarily give all the meanings of a word but focus on particular ones.

I also include, along with some general words, more difficult vocabulary which can give rise to problems. Learned words (*mots savants*) are a case in point.

Words lead naturally to idiomatic expressions. These may be simple turns of phrase or traditional idioms, still valid and vivid, or more recent ones.

I hope the selection will encourage ambitious students and interest teachers and others who work professionally with French. It is also for knowledgeable enthusiasts who wish to keep up the language, and for those people living or working in France whose first language is English. I hope their browsing will be rewarding.

C. K-G

Acknowledgements

My thanks go to Virginie Lavie, sometime *assistante* at Eastbourne College, for kindly making time to look through my first draft. I am also grateful to Nathalie Maupeu, then teaching at Moira House School, for diligently checking the bulk of my new version. Her comments were most valuable. Thanks too go to Simon Packard for some helpful suggestions. I am again grateful to Joan Wildman of JW Secretarial, Eastbourne, for her help.

My main reference book has been the 1998 *Collins Robert French Dictionary* (5th edition). It has also been useful to be able to consult at times *Dictionnaire des Expressions et Locutions Figurées* by Alain Rey and Sophie Chantreau (les usuels du Robert, 1979) and *Dictionnaire des Expressions* by Bruno Lafleur (Editions du Renouveau Pédagogique Inc., Ottawa, Canada, 1979 and Bordas, Paris, 1984).

A

An asterisk* denotes more familiar French

aberrant – ridiculous, preposterous:
e.g., Et maintenant on refuse de me rembourser. C'est **aberrant**. –
And now they refuse to reimburse me. It's quite absurd.
des prix aberrants – ridiculous prices.

abîme (m) – abyss;
être au bord de l'abîme (du gouffre) – to be on the verge of utter
despair:
e.g., nous **sommes au bord de l'abîme** – ruin is staring us in the
face.

abonder:
e.g., **abonder** dans le sens de quelqu'un – to be in complete
agreement with someone.

aboutir – to succeed, end successfully:
e.g., malheureusement ces discussions à haut niveau n'**ont** pas
abouti – Unfortunately these high-level discussions came to
nothing.

accélérateur (m);
donner un coup d'accélérateur – to speed things up:
e.g., l'affaire traîne toujours. Où est **le coup d'accélérateur** promis?
– The affair is dragging on. Where is the promised effort to speed
things up?

accident (m);
accident cardiaque – heart attack;
les accidents de la vie – life's unpleasant surprises and hardships
(including illness).

s'accorder avec – to go with (wine):
e.g., je trouve que ce vin **s'accorde** bien **avec** cette sole – I find that
this wine goes well with this sole.

acmé (f) – summit:
e.g., ce genre de comédie a connu **son acmé** pendant la guerre –
this sort of comedy reached its peak during the war.

à-coup (m) – jolt:
e.g., pour le moment ces recherches progressent sans **à-coups** – for
the moment this research is going along smoothly.

acte (m);
passer aux actes – to take action;
e.g., enfin le ministre **passe aux actes** – at last the minister is
taking action.

actif (m) – credit;
avoir à son actif – to have to one's credit, under one's belt:
e.g.,elle **a** plusieurs livres à succès **à son actif** – she has several
best-sellers to her credit;
ce gosse **a** déjà quelques vols **à son actif** – this kid has already a
number of thefts to his name.

active (f) – regular army.

activité (f) – job;
e.g., aller de **l'activité** à la retraite peut être dur – going from work
to retirement can be hard.

adepte (m/f) – fan, follower, devotee;
les adeptes du skate – skateboarding fans.

adhésion (f) – membership (club):
e.g., nous allons lancer une campagne **d'adhésion** – we are going to
launch a membership drive.

A D M (f);
les **A D M** – W M D (from **a**rmes de **d**estruction **m**assive –
weapons of **m**ass **d**estruction).

adostar (f)*:
e.g., c'est une **adostar** – he or she is a teenage star.

affabulation (f) – untruth, fabrication:
e.g., ce sont des **affabulations** – you can't believe a word of it.

affaire (f):
e.g., toutes **affaires** cessantes – forthwith, dropping everything else;
ce n'est pas une mince **affaire** – it's no easy task, it's no small
matter.

affranchir *;
affranchir quelqu'un – to brief someone, put in the know;
e.g., Pierre est arrivé le soir pour nous **affranchir**, ayant semé le
type qui le suivait – Pierre arrived in the evening to brief us, having
shaken off the chap who was tailing him.

s'affranchir de – to free oneself from;
s'affranchir du train-train quotidien – to free oneself from the
daily grind (routine).

affût (m);
être à l'affût de – to be on the lookout for:
e.g., elle **est** toujours **à l'affût d**'une occasion – she always has an
eye open for a bargain.

s'agglutiner – to congregate:
e.g., le soir de la finale toute la famille **s'agglutine** devant le
téléviseur – on the night of the final the whole family gathers round
the television.

agiter – to worry:
e.g., c'est un problème qui **agite** surtout les jeunes – young people
in particular worry about this problem.

aide (f) **juridictionelle** – legal aid.

aigrefin (m) – swindler, 'shark'.

aile (f);
battre de l'aile – to be in difficulties:
e.g., la sidérurgie **bat de l'aile** – the steel industry is struggling;
leur mariage **bat de l'aile** – their marriage is on the rocks.

alambiqué – over-subtle, finespun:
e.g., je trouve sa façon d'expliquer les choses un peu trop
alambiquée – I find his way of explaining things a bit too complicated.

alarme (f) **anti-effraction** – burglar alarm.

aléa (m) – vagary:
e.g., les **aléas** du temps anglais – the uncertainties of the English weather.

alerte (f) **à la bombe** – bomb scare.

allant (m) – dash, go, energy, zip:
e.g., il perd son **allant** – he is running out of steam.

alléchant – attractive:
e.g., les prix sont **alléchants** – the prices are tempting.

allée (f);
les allées/couloirs du pouvoir – the corridors of power.

alterné;
circulation alternée – contraflow.

amalgame (m);
faire l'amalgame – to lump together:
e.g., il ne faut pas **faire l'amalgame** entre les millionnaires et les gens aisés – you must not lump together the millionaires and those who are comfortably off;
e.g., faut pas **faire l'amalgame** – don't confuse the two.

amateur (m) – volunteer, taker:
e.g., 'Alors, qui sont **les amateurs** ici?' dit-elle, les torchons à la main – 'So, who is going to volunteer?' she said, dishcloths in hand.

américaine (f) *;
une grosse américaine – a big American car.

amour (m):
e.g., ce n'est pas **le grand amour** entre ces deux acteurs – there is no love lost between these two actors.

ancienneté (f) – seniority.

anguille (f):
e.g., il y a **anguille** sous roche – there's something suspicious going on, I smell a rat, there's more to it than meets the eye.

animalerie (f) – pet shop.

annoncé:
e.g., pour nous c'était le désastre **annoncé** – for us it was the disaster we saw coming.

antécédent (m):
e.g., c'était un bon élève sans **antécédents** – he was a good pupil with no previous history.

antenne (f) – branch, office;
e.g., nous avons des **antennes** tout le long de la côte – we have branches all along the coast.

anthologie (f):
e.g., Quel match! Un but d'**anthologie** – What a match! A classic goal.

anticipé – early;
retraite anticipée – early retirement.

antiémeutes;
unité antiémeutes – riot squad.

antitussif (m) – cough mixture.

aplanir – to smooth over;
e.g., je suis là pour **aplanir** les problèmes – I'm the troubleshooter.

apothicaire (m);
des comptes d'apothicaire – intricate calculations.

appareil (m);
dans le plus simple appareil – in the nude, wearing nothing.

appréciable – pleasant:
e.g., un week-end dans un hôtel de luxe serait **appréciable** – a weekend in a luxury hotel would be nice.

argent (m);
argent frais – ready cash;
l'argent est roi – money talks;
point d'argent point de Suisse – nothing for nothing (a reference to the Swiss mercenaries in times past).

arrêt (m);
un arrêt de travail – a sick note;
être en arrêt-maladie – to be off sick.

arrêter quelqu'un – to drop someone off:
e.g., je lui ai demandé de m'**arrêter** au coin de la rue – I asked him to drop me at the corner;
arrêter une date au crayon – to pencil in a date.

arrière (f);
assurer ses arrières – to cover one's back; leave oneself an escape route.

arrivée (f);
à l'arrivée – at the end of the day:
e.g., **à l'arrivée** le gouvernement n'a pas fait grand-chose pour les retraités – at the end of the day the government hasn't done much for retired people.

art (m);
dans les règles de l'art – properly, expertly:
e.g., ils ont pris tous les bijoux sans alerter personne et sans laisser de traces. Un 'casse' dans **les règles de l'art** – They took all the jewels without disturbing anyone and left no trace. A thoroughly professional job.

s'assagir – to quieten down, calm down:
e.g., enfin le temps **s'assagit** un peu – at last the weather is settling down a bit.

assainir;
assainir l'atmosphère – to clear the air:
e.g., j'y vais pour **assainir l'atmosphère** – I'm going there to clear the air.

assaut (m);
prendre d'assaut – to assault, storm:
e.g., en été ces restaurants chic au bord de la mer **sont pris d'assaut** – in summer these smart restaurants by the sea are swamped with people.

assorti;
être assorti de – to be accompanied by:
e.g., il peut s'attendre à une réprimande **assortie d'**une amende – he can expect a reprimand along with a fine.

assumer – to take responsibility for something, accept the situation:
e.g., nous avons eu des problèmes. Je suis le directeur. **J'assume** – We've had problems. I'm the headmaster. I accept responsibility (the buck stops with me).

assurer * – to be very competent, know what one is doing:
e.g., c'est en effet une personne timide mais dans la salle de classe il **assure** – he is in fact a shy person but in the classroom he really performs.

atout (m) – asset:
e.g., nous avons un autre **atout**; c'est qu'il fait très doux ici en hiver – we have another strong point; the very mild winter weather here.

attaquer – to sue (for **attaquer en justice**);
e.g., il était furieux et il a même pensé à **attaquer** sa banque – he was furious and he even thought of taking his bank to court.

attentat (m) – attack;
attentat suicide – suicide bomb attack.

attente (f);
une solution d'attente – a provisional solution.

attribuer:
e.g., ce numéro (de téléphone) n'est pas **attribué** – this number is not listed, recognised.

augmenter;
augmenter quelqu'un – to give someone a (pay) rise.

aune (f):
e.g., ces chiffres sont encourageants à **l'aune** de ceux du dernier rapport – these figures are encouraging put against those of the last report (**aune** was a form of measurement).

aurore (f);
aux aurores – at the crack of dawn.

aval (m) – backing:
e.g., il est impossible de procéder sans **l'aval** du maire – it is impossible to proceed without the mayor's backing.

avaler;
avaler les obstacles – to take obstacles in one's stride:
e.g., il ne manque pas de confiance. Il est sûr qu'il **avalera** tous **les obstacles** – he is not short of confidence. He is sure he'll easily cope with every obstacle.

avancée (f) – progress:
e.g., nous en avons parlé toute la matinée mais il n'y a pas d'**avancée** – we have been talking all morning but we haven't got anywhere.

s'avérer – to turn out:
e.g., le problème **s'est avéré** fort difficile – the problem turned out to be a very difficult one.

avertissement (m);
avertissement sans frais – clear warning:
e.g., **avertissement sans frais**. N'y revenez pas! – You've been warned. Don't do it again!

B

b-a ba (m);
être au b-a ba – to be at the initial stage:
e.g., l'agriculture biologique n'en **était** alors qu'**au b-a ba** – organic farming was then still in its very early stages.

baguette (f);
mener quelqu'un à la baguette – to rule someone with a rod of iron, be a hard taskmaster.

bal (m);
ouvrir le bal/la danse – to open the proceedings, start things off:
e.g., les meilleurs escrimeurs seront là mais c'est les juniors qui vont **ouvrir le bal** – the top fencers will be there but it's the juniors who will set the ball rolling.

balancer:
e.g., mon coeur **balance** entre la coupe de champagne et le martini – I can't make up my mind between a glass of champagne and a martini.

balancier (m);
un retour du balancier – a backlash, swing of the pendulum.

ban (m):
e.g., un **ban** pour le chef! – a round of applause for the chef! Let's hear it for the chef!
le prince était là avec le **ban** et l'arrière-**ban** de sa famille – the prince was there with all the various members of his family.

banc (m):
e.g., regagner les **bancs** de l'école – to return to school;
le ministère des Transports est sur le **banc** des accusés – the Ministry of Transport is in the dock.

banditisme (m);
le grand banditisme – serious crime.

baroud (m);
baroud d'honneur – last defiant stand.

barque (f);
bien mener sa barque – to manage one's affairs well.

barre (f);
mettre la barre plus haut – to raise the bar:
e.g., c'était un professeur stimulant qui voulait toujours **mettre la barre plus haut** – he was an inspirational teacher who always wanted to set even higher standards.

barre (f);
redresser la barre – to get back on course:
e.g., le gouvernement a été assez secoué mais le Premier ministre a pu **redresser la barre** – the government was somewhat shaken but the Prime Minister has succeeded in steadying the ship.

barre (f);
barre à mine – crowbar.

barrière (f);
barrière de sécurité – crush barrier.

base (f);
jeter les bases – to lay the foundations:
e.g., ils sont en train de **jeter les bases** de leur nouvelle politique étrangère – they are laying the foundations of their new foreign policy.

bataille (f);
bataille rangée – pitched battle;
garer sa voiture en bataille – to park one's car at an angle, diagonally;
les cheveux en bataille – wild, untidy hair.

battant (m) – go-getter, go-ahead character.

baume (m);
donner/mettre du baume au coeur – to console, comfort.

bémol (m);
mettre un bémol – to lower the tone, ease up:
e.g., certains ont un peu trop réagi et il est temps de **mettre un bémol** – some have overreacted a bit and it is time to quieten things down.

berne (f);
être en berne – to be at half-mast;
avoir le moral en berne – to be downhearted, in low spirits, down in the dumps.

berner – to deceive;
se faire berner – to be taken in, conned.

besoin (m);
si besoin s'en fait sentir – should the need arise.

bétonnage (m) – concreting over, overdevelopment (with the implication of beauty spots being covered with new buildings).

beuverie (f) – drinking session;
la beuverie du week-end – week-end binge drinking.

bilan (m);
faire le bilan – to size up:
e.g., c'est peut-être le moment de **faire le bilan** de ma vie – it is perhaps time to take stock of my life.

bio* – organic (from **biologique**):
e.g., ma belle-mère achète toujours du **bio** – my mother-in-law is into organic food.

blanc-seing (m) – blank cheque, free hand;
il se trompe s'il croit que le président va lui donner un **blanc-seing** – he's mistaken if he thinks that the President is going to give him a blank cheque.

blanchiment (m);
blanchiment d'argent – money laundering.

blanchir – to find innocent;
être blanchi par la justice – to be cleared by the courts.

blouse (f);
les blouses blanches * – medics (the image of them in their white coats).

bob (m) – sunhat.

boisseau (m);
tenir/mettre sous le boisseau – to keep secret:
e.g., c'est une qualité qu'elle a préféré **mettre sous le boisseau** – it's a quality which she has preferred to keep hidden away (**boisseau** = bushel).

boiter;
l'industrie boite bas – industry is struggling (**boiter bas** – to have a noticeable limp).

bombe (f);
c'est une bombe à retardement – it's a time bomb:
e.g., et si cette manufacture d'armes prenait feu? Pour beaucoup de gens **c'est une bombe à retardement** – and what if this munitions factory caught fire? For many people it's an accident waiting to happen.

bord (m):
e.g., il est un peu fanfaron sur les **bords** * – he's a bit of a boaster.

bouché – overcast:
e.g., malheureusement le ciel est resté **bouché** – unfortunately it has remained overcast.

boucle (f);
e.g., dans le hall d'arrivée on diffusait en **boucle** le même message – in the arrivals' hall the same message was being broadcast continuously;
la boucle est bouclée – we have come full circle.

boucler;
boucler une rue – to cordon off a street.

bouclier (m);
une levée de boucliers – an uproar, (to be) up in arms:
e.g., ces mesures draconiennes vont sans doute provoquer **une levée de boucliers –** these draconian measures will doubtless cause a great outcry.

bouée (f);
lancer une bouée de sauvetage/secours – to throw a lifeline:
e.g., je ne l'oublierai jamais. C'est lui qui **m'a lancé une bouée de sauvetage** lorsque je traversais une mauvaise passe – I'll never forget him. He was the one who threw me a lifeline when I was going through a bad patch.

bougonner – to grumble.

boule (f);
boules Quiès – earplugs.

boulet (m);
sentir (passer) le vent du boulet – to have a narrow escape:
e.g., de plus, leur patron aurait pu faire venir la police. Les deux employés **ont senti passer le vent du boulet** – Furthermore the boss could have called the police. For the two employees it was a close thing;
tirer à boulets rouges (sur) – to criticize harshly:
e.g., après cet incident à l'école la presse **a tiré à boulets rouges** sur le directeur – after this incident at the school the press hammered the headmaster;
traîner un boulet – to have a millstone round one's neck:
e.g., j'espère que je ne vais pas **traîner ce boulet** toute ma vie – I hope I'm not going to have this millstone around my neck all my life.

boulon (m);
serrer les boulons – to tighten things up:
e,g., les temps sont difficiles et la direction a donné l'ordre de **serrer les boulons** – times are difficult and management has given orders to tighten things up.

bourreau (m);
bourreau de travail – glutton for work, workaholic.

bout (m);
du bout des lèvres – half-heartedly:
e,g., elle m'a félicité **du bout des lèvres** – her congratulations were
less than warm;
prendre quelque chose par le bon bout – to go about something
the right way.

box(m);
box (fermé) – lock-up (garage).

braquer:
e.g., un refus impoli m'**aurait braqué** – an impolite refusal would
have put my back up;
il **est braqué** contre tous les changements que je propose – he is
dead set against all my proposed changes.

brève (f) – short news item (newspapers).

bride (f);
à bride abattue – hell for leather, at full tilt:
e.g., les trois voyous ont descendu les marches **à bride abattue** –
the three hooligans came hurtling down the steps;
laisser la bride sur le cou à quelqu'un – to allow someone a free
hand:
e.g., qu'est ce qu'on veut exactement? La bonne discipline ou **la bride
sur le cou**? – What do we want exactly? Good discipline or do as
you please?
tenir la bride haute – to keep a firm hand:
e.g., au début il **a tenu la bride haute** à sa jeune équipe – to begin
with he kept a tight rein on his young team;
tourner bride – to about-turn:
e.g., voyant le barrage de police les émeutiers **ont tourné bride** –
seeing the police cordon the rioters turned tail.

bridger – to play bridge;
bridgeur (m),

bridgeuse (f) – bridge player.

brocarder (quelqu'un) – to taunt (literary).

bronca (f) – jeers:
e.g., l'arbitre a été accueilli par une **bronca** – the referee was greeted by boos.

bronzer – to sunbathe, get a tan:
e.g., il ne faut pas **bronzer** idiot – you mustn't overdo the sunbathing.

brouille (f) – quarrel, row.

buter – to stumble:
e.g., sur quoi **butent** les pourparlers cette fois? – what is the sticking point this time?

butoir (m);
date butoir/limite – deadline.

C

cabanon (m) – shed;
cabanon de jardin – garden shed.

Caddie (m) – trolley (supermarket, airport).

cadeau (m);
ne pas faire de cadeau – not to make any concessions, to do no favours:
e.g., son patron **ne fait pas de cadeau** – his boss is uncompromising.
cadeau empoisonné – poisoned chalice.

cadrer – to tally, square (with):
e.g., sa réputation d'un homme dur ne **cadre** pas avec sa générosité envers les défavorisés – his reputation as a hard man does not fit in with his generosity to those who have little.

cagnotte (f) – kitty:
e.g., la **cagnotte** est de 10,000 livres – the kitty has £10,000 in it.

cagoulard (m) – hooded person, or someone wearing a mask of some sort:
e.g., plus tôt, j'avais vu deux **cagoulards** y entrer – earlier I had seen two hooded figures go in there.

cagoulé (also **encagoulé**) – wearing a hood or mask.

calciner – to burn out:
e.g., une vieille voiture **calcinée** – a burnt-out old car.

calicot (m) – banner:
e.g., j'ai bien vu leur **calicot** mais sans vraiment comprendre leur slogan – I saw their banner all right but without really understanding their slogan.

camp (m):
marquer contre son propre **camp** – to score an own goal.

cap (m);
e,g., elle vient de passer le **cap** de ses 50 ans – she has just had her fiftieth birthday;
changer de cap – to change course;
tenir le cap – to keep on course.

capharnaüm (m) * – chaos, confusion:
e.g., la situation tourne au **capharnaüm** – the situation is becoming chaotic.

caractérisé – clear cut:
e.g., c'est de l'effronterie **caractérisée** – it's downright cheek.

carcéral;
la surpopulation carcérale – the overcrowding in prisons.

caritatif – charitable:
e.g., un cocktail **caritatif** – a charity drinks party.

carré (m);
le dernier carré – the remaining few:
e.g., quant aux fêtards il n'en restait que **le dernier carré** – as for the revellers only the last few remained.

carreau (m);
se tenir à carreau * – to tread carefully:
e.g., si c'est votre première visite n'oubliez pas que la police là-bas est très vigilante. Il faut **vous tenir à carreau** – if you're visiting for the first time don't forget that the police there are very vigilant. You must watch how you go.

carte (f);
carte maîtresse – trump card:
e.g., la **carte maîtresse** de l'avocat de la défense a tout changé – the defense counsel's trump card changed everything;
abattre ses cartes/son jeu – to put one's cards on the table.
dévoiler ses cartes/son jeu – to show one's hand;

cas (m);
au cas par cas – individually, each case on its own merits;
cas d'espèce – particular case;
cas de figure – scenario:
e.g., selon moi il y a deux **cas de figure** possibles dont l'un est plus agréable que l'autre – in my view there are two possible scenarios of which one is nicer than the other.
cas limite – borderline case.

casier (m) **judiciaire** (vierge) – (clean) (police) record.

Cassandre (f);
jouer les Cassandre – to be a prophet of doom.

casse-cou (m);
crier casse-cou – to sound a warning note:
e.g., les médecins **ont crié casse-cou**. Le jogging n'est pas pour tout le monde – doctors have sounded a warning note. Jogging is not for everyone.

casseur (m) – demonstrator (bent on trouble and violence).

catastrophe (f)
catastrophe naturelle – Act of God.

caviar (m);
la gauche caviar – champagne socialists.

cécité (f) – blindness.

cendre (f);
couver sous la cendre – to be simmering away:
e.g., un sentiment de mécontentement **couve sous la cendre** – a
feeling of discontent is simmering away.
remuer les cendres – to rake over the ashes:
e.g., ils sont vieux maintenant, nous aussi. À quoi bon **remuer les
cendres**? – They are old now, so are we. What's the point in raking
over the ashes?

centrale (f) – 1. power station (for **centrale électrique**);
                  2. prison:
e.g., **centrale de longue détention** – long-term jail.

chaîne (f);
chaîne hertzienne – terrestrial channel (TV).

chapeauter – to oversee:
e.g., tous les sports de plein air ici **sont chapeautés** par un
entraîneur expérimenté – all the outdoor sports here are headed by
an experienced coach.

chapitrer – to rebuke.

charentaise (f) – (comfortable) slipper:
e.g., tu prends ta retraite, alors? T'es prêt à enfiler les **charentaises**?
– So you're retiring? You're all ready to put on your slippers?

charge (f);
charge de travail – work load.

charivari (m) – confused din, commotion.

charme (m);
hôtel de charme – pleasant hotel of character, privately run;
photo de charme – sexy photograph, 'page 3' picture.

chasuble (f);
chasuble fluorescente – (sleeveless) fluorescent jacket:
e.g., des policiers en **chasuble fluorescente** – policemen wearing
fluorescent jackets (a variant on the usual **gilet fluorescent**).

chaud;
à chaud – on the spot (e.g., reporters):
e.g., ses commentaires **à chaud** sur la guerre étaient bien connus –
her on-the-spot commentaries on the war were well known;
il ne faut jamais trahir un copain ou ça vous coûtera **chaud** * – you
must never betray a pal or it'll cost you dear.
chaude alerte * – a close call;

chemin (m);
passer son chemin – to go one's way:
e.g., il est trop facile de **passer son chemin** – it is too easy to pass
by on the other side.

cher:
e.g., ne pas donner **cher** de ses chances – not to give much for one's
chances.

cheville ouvrière (f) – kingpin:
e.g., c'est une petite maison d'édition et c'est Louise qui en est la
cheville ouvrière – it's a small publishing company and it all
revolves round Louise here.

chèvre (f);
ménager la chèvre et le chou – to run with the hare and hunt
with the hounds:
cela lui plaît de **ménager la chèvre et le chou** mais cela comporte
des risques – he likes to play along with both sides but it's a risky
thing to do.

chien (m);
être couché en chien de fusil – to be lying curled up:
e.g., il regarda longuement le corps **couché en chien de fusil** sur le tapis tacheté de sang – he looked for a long time at the body curled up on the blood-stained carpet.

chimérique;
un rêve chimérique – a pipe dream.

choc (m);
choc en retour – backlash;
un choc en retour de la haine – a backlash of hatred.

chômage (m);
en chômage technique – laid off.

chômer:
jour chômé – bank holiday.

chou (m);
faire chou blanc – to draw a blank:
e.g., malgré tous leurs efforts les policiers **ont fait chou blanc** – in spite of all their efforts the detectives have drawn a blank.
faire ses choux gras (de quelque chose) – to do well (out of something):
e.g., la presse **a fait ses choux gras** de ce scandale – the press has had a field day with this scandal.

chronique (f);
défrayer la chronique – to be a big news item, front-page news:
e.g., pendant les années 50 la vie de ces deux vedettes **a défrayé la chronique** – during the '50s the life of those two stars was much in the news.

chuter – to fall:
e.g., elle **chuta** de son vélo – she fell off her bike.
faire chuter le taux de cholésterol – to bring down the cholesterol level.

cimetière (m);
cimetière de voitures – scrapyard (**cimetière =** cemetery).

clair;
passer le plus clair de son temps (**à faire quelque chose**) – to
spend most of one's time (doing something):
e.g., leur grand-mère **passe le plus clair de son temps à** tricoter –
their grandmother spends most of her time knitting.

claque (f) – slap:
e.g., ils ont refusé. Nous avons pris une **claque**, ce jour-là – They
refused. It was a slap in the face for us, that day.

clé (f);
à la clé – added on, in addition:
e.g., un travail avec un bonus **à la clé** – a job with a bonus at the
end.

clignotant (m) – warning light:
e.g., quant à l'économie tous les **clignotants** sont au rouge – as for
the economy all the warning lights are flashing red.

clim (f) * – air con, air conditioning (from **climatisation**).

cocooner:
e,g., je vais **cocooner** chez moi – I'm going to snuggle down at
home.

coeur (m);
avoir un coup de coeur pour quelque chose – to fall in love
with, fall for something:
e.g., voici la liste de nos cocktails **coup de coeur** – here is the list of
our top cocktails.

collectif;
les sports collectifs – team sports.

co-location (f) – (rented) flat sharing. (It may also be **co-loc** *,
especially in student-speak.)

comète (f);
tirer des plans sur la comète * – to indulge in far-fetched dreams and hopes.

commanditaire (m) – sponsor, backer, organiser:
e.g., plusieurs hommes ont été interpellés mais le **commanditaire** est toujours recherché – several men have been taken in by the police but the person behind it all is still being sought.

comminatoire – threatening;
un ton comminatoire – a threatening tone.

commun;
les transports en commun – public transport;
il n'y a pas de commune mesure entre ces deux événements – there is no comparison between these two events.

compte;
y trouver son compte – to gain something, do well:
e.g., comme ça, tout le monde **y trouve son compte** – in that way everyone is a winner, everyone gets something out of it.

compte-gouttes (m);
au compte-gouttes – in dribs and drabs:
e.g., la guerre finie, les touristes reviennent **au compte-gouttes** – with the war over tourists are trickling back.

conditionnel;
prendre au conditionnel – not to take as confirmed:
e.g., l'accident est grave mais ces chiffres sont à **prendre au conditionnel** – it's a serious accident but these figures are unconfirmed.

confronter – to compare:
e.g., pour commencer, nous avons **confronté** les deux versions – to begin with we compared the two versions.

confusion (f);
confusion des peines – sentences to run concurrently (legal).

se **connecter** sur – to log on (computer).

conter:
e.g., ne pas s'en laisser **conter** – not to be easily fooled, not to let oneself be duped so easily.

contraint et forcé – under duress.

contrecoup (m) – repercussion(s), after-effects.

contre-pied;
prendre à contre-pied – to wrong-foot;
e.g., le gouvernement se trouve **pris à contre-pied** – the government finds itself caught on the wrong foot.

contrevérité (f) – untruth.

contrôle (m) **continu** – continuous assessment.

coordonnées (f) – personal details;
e.g., si vous voulez bien me donner vos **coordonnées** on vous écrira – if you'd like to give me your particulars somebody will write to you.

copie (f);
revoir sa copie – to come up with a better version (the expression has echoes of the classroom):
e.g., une bonne idée, certes, mais dans la pratique il y a trop de difficultés. Le fisc doit **revoir sa copie** – a good idea, certainly, but in practice there are too many difficulties. The tax people must rework the idea.

copinage (m); *
copinage politique – political cronyism.

corde (f);
tenir la corde – to have the advantage, edge;
être sur la corde raide – to walk a tightrope, be on the high wire, in a difficult position.

correspondre à – to suit:
e.g., peut-être que cette méthode de paiement vous **correspondra**
mieux – perhaps this method of payment will suit you better.

cossu – rich, well-heeled;
un quartier cossu – a well-off neighbourhood.

cote (f);
avoir la cote – to be in favour, well thought of:
e.g., malgré cette crise le Premier ministre **a** toujours **la cote** – in
spite of this crisis the Prime Minister is still popular.
Sa **cote** est en baisse – she is not as popular as she was.

couchage (m):
e.g., 6 **couchages** – sleeps 6 (as in advertisements for holiday
homes).

coude (m);
être au coude à coude – to be neck and neck;
jouer des coudes – to elbow one's way:
e.g., J'ai dû **jouer des coudes** pour arriver au bar – I had to fight
my way to the bar.

coudée (f);
avoir ses coudées franches – to have elbow room, room to
manoeuvre, not to be hemmed in.

couleuvre (f);
avaler des couleuvres – 1. to put up with insults, suffer
humiliation in silence;
　　　　　　　　　　　　　　　2. to swallow a lie, be duped.

coupe (f);
coupes claires/sombres – axing, severe cuts:
e.g., reste à savoir s'ils pourront éviter de faire des **coupes sombres**
– it remains to be seen whether they'll be able to avoid making
drastic cuts.

cour (f);
jouer dans la cour des grands – to be a top player, be up with the big boys:
e.g., il est parti de rien. Aujourd'hui c'est un homme d'affaires important qui **joue dans la cour des grands** – He started from nothing. Today he is an important businessman who is a major player. (The image is of the school playground.)

courant (m):
e.g., le **courant passe** entre les deux présidents – the two presidents hit it off.

couronne (f);
tresser des couronnes/lauriers à quelqu'un – to heap praise on someone.

cours (m);
cours accéléré – crash course;
cours de rattrapage – catch-up lessons.

course (f);
en bout de course – at the end of the day:
e.g., beaucoup de gens diront qu'**en bout de course** le gouvernement aurait pu mieux faire – many people will say that at the end of the day the government could have done better.

course-poursuite (f) – car chase (by police).

court;
tourner court – to come to an abrupt halt:
e.g., les négotiations **ont tourné court** ce matin – the negotiations stalled abruptly this morning.

covoiturage (m) – car sharing.

cran (m);
monter d'un cran – to go up a notch:
e.g., la tension **monte d'un cran** – the tension goes up a notch.

crédits (m) − funds:
e.g., au pire, ils pourraient nous couper les **crédits** − if the worst
comes to the worst they could cut off our funding.

créneau (m);
monter au créneau − to go into action, be quick to defend:
e.g., il est toujours prêt à **monter au créneau** pour aider ses amis −
he is always ready to go into battle to help his friends.

creuser;
creuser un thème − to go into a subject in depth.

criminalité (f);
la grande criminalité − serious crime.

critiquable − open to criticism;
conduite critiquable − conduct which is open to criticism.

croisière (f);
prendre/trouver son rythme de croisière − to get into one's
stride:
e.g., notre campagne **a trouvé** difficilement **son rythme de
croisière** − it has been difficult for our campaign to get into its
stride.

cru (m);
du cru − local:
e.g., les voyous **du cru** posent toujours des problèmes − the local
yobs are still causing problems.

culot (m) * − cheek, chutzpah:
e.g., ils y sont entrés au **culot** − they bluffed their way in.

culpabiliser − to feel guilty:
e.g., si je ne lui téléphone pas chaque jour je **culpabilise** − if I don't
phone her every day I feel guilty.

D

danse (f);
entrer dans la danse – to join in:
e.g., si un autre syndicat **entre dans la danse** maintenant, il ne
s'agira plus d'une crise mais d'un conflit – if another union joins
now, it will no longer be a crisis but a conflict.
mener la danse – to lead the way:
e.g., tous les élèves étaient mécontents et c'est le fils d'un professeur
qui **menait la danse** – all the pupils were dissatisfied and a
teacher's son was leading the way.

danseuse (f) – something on which you spend too much money:
e.g., on parle de construire une marina ici mais les gens sont contre
cette **danseuse** – there is talk of building a marina here but the
people are against this money-wasting project. (The word is also used
for extravagant passions and interests; the image goes back to the
other meaning of **danseuse** = a mistress on whom you lavish a lot of
money.)

faire date (f) – to stand out, be a landmark:
e.g., parmi les grands championnats celui-ci **fait date** – among the
great championships this one stands out.

débaucher – 1. to lay off (e.g. workforce):
e.g., il est inévitable qu'on **débauche** – people are bound to be laid
off;
débaucher quelqu'un – 2. to poach, lure away someone.

décalage (m) – gap:
e.g., il est en **décalage** avec les opinions des adolescents – he is out
of sync with teenagers' opinions;
décalage horaire – 1. time-difference;
                       2. jet-lag.

décanter – to settle down:
e.g., en attendant que les choses se **décantent** je ne bouge pas –
while waiting for things to settle down I'm staying put.

déceler – to reveal:
e.g., la radio pulmonaire n'**a** rien **décelé** – the lung X-ray was clear.

décharge (f) – 1. discharge:
e.g., **décharge électrique** – electric shock;
        – 2. rubbish tip:
e.g., c'est bon pour la **décharge** – it can be thrown away.

décor (m);
l'envers du décor – the other side of the picture:
e.g., Le quartier est coquet mais il y a **l'envers du décor**. Trop des jeunes ici tombent dans la petite délinquence – the neighbourhood is neat and trim but there is another side. Too many of the young here fall into petty crime.

décortiquer – to dissect;
décortiquer les événements – to analyse what is happening in detail.

découdre;
en découdre avec quelqu'un – to cross swords with someone:
e.g., elle est toujours prête à **en découdre avec** la bureaucratie – she is always ready to take on officialdom.

décrisper – to defuse;
décrisper la situation – to defuse the situation.

dédouaner – to clear:
e.g., finalement, après la guerre, on l'**a dédouané** – finally, after the war, his name was cleared.

se dégrader:
e.g., le temps **se dégrade** – the weather is breaking up, getting worse.

dégraissage (m) – slimming down of the workforce, reduction in personnel.

déguisement (m) – 1. disguise;
2. fancy dress:
e.g., un concours de **déguisements** – a fancy-dress competition.

délestage (m) – 1. power cut;
2. diversion (traffic).

délictuel – criminal;
traffic d'armes délictuel – illegal trafficking of arms.

délinquant (m), **déliquante** (f);
délinquant sexuel – sex offender.

délit (m);
délit d'initié – insider trading.

délocalisation (f) – relocation.

demandeur (m), **demandeuse** (f);
demandeur d'emploi – job seeker.

démarchage (m);
démarchage téléphonique – cold calling.

se démentir – to fail, fade:
e.g., une passion qui ne **s'est** jamais **démentie** – a passion which is as strong as ever.

démériter:
e.g., n'oublions pas les juniors qui n'**ont** pas **démérité** – don't let us forget the junior players who have not done badly at all.

demi-teinte (f):
e.g., un début de saison en **demi-teinte** pour nos basketteurs – an uneven beginning for our basketball players;
une année en demi-teinte – a so-so year.

se démobiliser – to become dejected, lose motivation:
e.g., il leur faut surtout éviter de **se démobiliser** après un tel échec
– they must above all avoid becoming demoralized after such a
setback.

démordre:
e.g., elle n'en **démord** pas – she's sticking to her guns.

denier (m);
payer de ses (propres) deniers – to pay up out of one's own
pocket.

denrée (f);
devenir une denrée rare – to become a rare commodity:
e.g., autre chose, il me semble que la loyauté **devient** de nos jours
une denrée rare – another thing, it seems to me that loyalty
nowadays is becoming a rare commodity.

dent (f);
garder une dent (contre) – to bear a grudge (against):
e.g., il semble **garder une dent contre** tout le monde – he seems to
have a chip on his shoulder.

déparer – to spoil;
déparer le paysage – to spoil the countryside.

dépénaliser – to decriminalize.

dépistage (m) – screening (medical):
e.g., un test de **dépistage** du Sida – a screening test for Aids.

se déprendre de – to lose one's affection for:
e.g., un collègue dont elle **se déprenait** – a colleague of whom she
was no longer so fond.

déprogrammer – to take off, cancel (TV).

dernier;
le petit dernier – 1. latest, youngest (boy);
2. last drink, perhaps a post-meal cognac *:
e.g., de plus en plus de gens ont supprimé **le petit dernier** – more and more people have cut out that last little drink.

désamorcer – to defuse;
désamorcer une crise – to defuse a crisis.

se désapprendre (à) – to forget (how to):
e.g., ces enfants, qui ont beaucoup souffert, **se sont désappris à** tenir une conversation – these children, who have suffered a lot, have forgotten how to have a conversation.

désarmer:
e.g., mon patron répète le même argument. Il ne **désarme** pas – my boss repeats the same argument. He is not backing down.

désaveu (m) – retraction, denial, rejection, snub.

désemparer;
sans désemparer – without stopping:
e.g., ils luttent contre les flammes **sans désemparer** – it's a non-stop struggle against the flames.

désemplir;
e.g., ce restaurant ne **désemplit** pas depuis l'arrivée de ce chef – this restaurant is always full since this chef arrived.

désert (m);
la traversée du désert – the political wilderness (or in a general sense):
e.g., est-ce-que le tennis britannique est sur le point de sortir de **sa traversée du désert**? – is British tennis about to emerge from its difficult period?

se désinhiber – to lose one's inhibitions.

dessus (m);
prendre le dessus – to get the upper hand:
e.g., la semaine prochaine le mauvais temps va **prendre le dessus** – next week the bad weather is going to dominate.

diable (m);
tenter le diable – to tempt fate:
e.g., il y a toujours la possibilité d'un contrôle inopiné. Je ne veux pas **tenter le diable** – there's always the chance of a spot check. I don't want to tempt fate.

dialoguer – to hold talks:
e.g., je ne sais pas s'ils sont prêts à **dialoguer** avec le gouvernement – I don't know if they are willing to hold talks with the government.

diapason (m);
être au diapason (de) – to be in tune (with):
e.g., il a 50 ans mais il prétend **être au diapason des** jeunes – he is 50 but he claims to be in tune with the young.

discours-programme (m) – keynote speech.

disculper – to exonerate (as opposed to **inculper**).

se disqualifier – to lose credit:
e.g., en faisant cela il **s'est disqualifié** auprès de ses collègues – in doing that he has lowered himself in the eyes of his colleagues.

distinguer – to honour:
e.g., peut-être que la Reine va vous **distinguer** – perhaps the Queen will honour you.

dithyrambique (literary);
une critique dithyrambique – a rave review (otherwise the word is not common).

doigt (m);
montrer du doigt – to point the finger:
e.g., cette fois on **montre du doigt** les supermarchés – this time the finger is being pointed at supermarkets.

donne (f) – situation:
e.g., la mort d'un prisonnier a radicalement changé la **donne** – the
death of a prisoner has radically changed things.

se donner – to make a big effort, put something into it:
e.g., je me repose le week-end mais pendant la semaine **je me donne**
car mon boulot me passionne – I take it easy at the week-end but
during the week I really get down to it for I love my job.

doper – to stimulate, boost:
e.g., j'ai pensé à une astuce pour **doper** les ventes – I've thought of
a clever idea to stimulate sales.

doser – to measure out:
e.g., le truc, c'est de savoir **doser** entre le travail et le plaisir – the
trick is to get the balance right between work and pleasure.

doux;
médecine douce – natural medicine.
prix doux – (as a French advertisement might say) prices you'll
like.

drainer – to attract:
e.g., cette exposition **draine** aussi beaucoup de touristes – this
exhibition also pulls in a lot of tourists.

drame (m) – tragedy:
e.g., le **drame**, c'est que les enfants aussi sont touchés – the tragedy
is that this affects children as well.

droit (m):
e.g., il n'a pas **droit** à l'erreur – he can't afford to get it wrong.
être dans son bon droit – to be within one's rights;
droit de garde – custody (of children).

dure (f);
coucher à/sur la dure – to sleep rough.

E

eau (f):
e.g., c'est clair comme **l'eau de roche** – it is crystal clear;
à l'eau de rose – sentimental:
e.g., un feuilleton **à l'eau de rose** – a sentimental soap.

ébauche (f) – rough draft;
être au stade de l'ébauche – to be at an early stage.

ébruiter – to spread (news), noise abroad, reveal:
e.g., mes rivaux n'ont pas tardé à **ébruiter** cette affaire – my rivals
did not take long to broadcast around this affair.

écart (m);
faire le grand écart – to do the splits:
e.g., je **fais** actuellement **le grand écart** entre les deux boulots – at
the moment I'm really stretched between the two jobs.

échauffourée (f) – skuffle, affray, skirmish (also military skirmish).

échec (m) – setback;
se solder par un échec – to end in failure, come to nothing;
les jeunes en situation d'échec scolaire – those who fail at
school.

échiquier (m);
échiquier politique – political landscape.

éclabousser – to besmirch:
e.g., il n'y a pas de doute que le général **a été éclaboussé** par ce
scandale de famille – there is no doubt that the general's good name
has suffered as a result of this family scandal.

éclipse (f):
e.g., j'ai loué son jardinier mais, selon elle, c'est un jardinier à
éclipses – I praised her gardener but, according to her, he is one
who comes and goes.

écoutes (f);
mettre quelqu'un sur écoutes – to tap someone's phone;
écoutes sauvages – illegal phone tapping.

écrit;
c'est écrit – it is fate:
e.g., un jour son fils millionnaire a perdu tout son argent. **C'était écrit** – One day her millionaire son lost all his money. It had to happen.

édulcorer – to sweeten, water down:
e.g., ce que vous lisez est une version **édulcorée** – what you are reading is a watered-down version.

effet (m);
effet de serre – greenhouse effect;
effets secondaires – side-effects.

égalité (f);
l'égalité des chances – equal opportunities.

égrener;
égrener (son chapelet de) – to reel off:
e.g., elle **a égrené le chapelet de** ses plaintes – she reeled off all her complaints.

élongation (f) – pulled muscle;
e.g., il est victime d'**une élongation** – he is suffering from a pulled muscle.

s'embêter avec – to bother oneself with:
e.g., les gens achètent ces appartements chic parce qu'ils ne veulent plus **s'embêter avec** l'entretien d'une maison – people are buying these smart flats because they can no longer be bothered with looking after a house.

embouché;
mal embouché – foul-mouthed.

émoulu;
frais émoulu de l'université – fresh from, just out of, university.

empêcheur (m);
empêcheur de danser/tourner en rond – spoilsport:
e.g., est-ce-que l'Angleterre va opposer son veto et être l'**empêcheur de danser en rond**? – is England going to use its veto and be the party pooper?

s'employer à – to devote one's energies to:
e.g., la tâche est importante et le ministre **s'y emploie** – it's an important task and the minister is devoting his efforts to it.

encadrer – to train, instruct:
e.g., les soldats qui **encadrent** ces jeunes hommes sont des professionnels chevronnés – the soldiers who train these young men are seasoned professionals.

en-cas (m) – snack.

encenser – to praise highly, extol.

enchères (f);
faire monter les enchères – to raise the stakes, up the ante.

encombrement (m) – traffic jam, heavy traffic.

endiguer – to stem, contain:
e.g., leur problème, c'est comment **endiguer** le virus – their problem is how to contain the virus.

enfance (f):
e.g., c'est l'**enfance** de l'art – it's child's play.

enfoncer;
enfoncer un coin – to drive a wedge:
e.g., elle est jalouse. Elle cherche à **enfoncer un coin** dans notre amitié – She is jealous. She is trying to drive a wedge between us.

engouement (m) – infatuation, passion.

s'enliser – to get bogged down;
s'enliser dans des discussions – to get bogged down in discussions.

énormité (f) – howler.

entamer – 1. to begin:
e.g., les négotiations **sont** enfin **entamées** – the negotiations are at last under way;
        2. to damage:
e.g., ces ragots n'**ont** pas **entamé** sa popularité – this tittle-tattle has not harmed his popularity.

s'enticher de – to become infatuated with.

entier;
rester entier – to remain unresolved:
e.g., le mystère **reste entier** – the mystery is still unresolved.

entorse (f);
faire une entorse au règlement – to bend the rules.

enveloppe (f) – budget, allocated sum:
e.g., on espère que l'**enveloppe** sera plus généreuse cette fois – we are hoping for a more generous sum this time.

éoliennes (f) – wind farm (the French word sounds almost poetic – it comes from classical mythology: *Aeolus* (**Eole)** was the God of Winds).

épidermique;
une réaction épidermique – a knee-jerk reaction.

épingle (f);
monter en épingle – to blow up, exaggerate:
e.g., c'est un incident banal que la presse **a monté en épingle** – it's an ordinary incident blown up by the press;
tirer son épingle du jeu – to get out unscathed:
e.g., le président a agi vite et a pu **tirer son épingle du jeu** – the President acted quickly and was able to get out of the situation while the going was good.

épisodique – occasional:
e.g., et demain, des averses **épisodiques** – and tomorrow, the odd shower.

épreuve (f);
épreuve des tirs au but – penalty shoot-out.

ergothérapeute (m/f) – occupational therapist.

espèces (f) – cash:
e.g., ne joignez pas **d'espèces** – don't enclose any money (in the envelope).

espérance (f);
l'espérance de vie – life expectancy.

espoir (m):
e.g., tous **les espoirs** sont permis – we can be full of hope.

essai (m);
transformer l'essai – to capitalise on, build on the success achieved, press (home) one's advantage (literally, to convert a try in rugby).

étape (f);
brûler/griller * **les étapes** – to press on without stopping:
e.g., l'enquête n'est pas facile. Il faut procéder méthodiquement. Il n'est pas question **qu'on brûle les étapes** – the enquiry isn't an easy one. We must proceed methodically. There's no question of our cutting corners.

état (m);
état d'esprit – state of mind;
état second – daze:
e.g., j'étais dans **un état second** – I was in a daze;
avoir des états d'âme – to have doubts, reservations.

Eternel (m);
devant l'Eternel (used informally for emphasis):
e.g., c'est le grand organisateur **devant l'Eternel** – he is the great organiser.

étrier (m);
avoir le pied à l'étrier – to be on the way up:
e.g., son fils a maintenant une assez bonne position. Il **a le pied à l'étrier** ce qui rassure sa mère – her son has now quite a good job. He has a foot on the ladder (**étrier** – stirrup), which reassures his mother.

Evangile (m);
prendre pour parole d'Evangile – to take as gospel (truth).

évasion (f);
l'évasion fin juillet – the summer holiday getaway (France).

événement (m) – sensational (e.g., book or film);
un roman/film **événement** – a blockbuster;
les événements se précipitent – it's all happening in a rush.

évolutif;
un poste évolutif – a job with good prospects.

évolution (f):
e.g., selon l'annonce il y a la possibilité d'**évolution** rapide – according to the advertisement there is a chance of rapid promotion.

exactions (f) – (examples of) violence:
e.g., on a vraiment honte de telles **exactions** – one is really ashamed at such instances of violence.

examen (m);
se faire faire des examens – to have tests done (medical);
examens de contrôle – a check-up.

extraconjugal – extramarital.

excentré – away from the centre;
supermarchés excentrés – out-of-town supermarkets.

exergue (m);
mettre en exergue – to highlight:
e.g., cette histoire **met en exergue** les dangers d'une telle aventure
– this story emphasizes the dangers of such an adventure.

exploit (m):
e.g., trouver un taxi par mauvais temps relève de l'**exploit** – finding
a taxi in bad weather is a veritable feat.

F

fable (f) – made-up story:
e.g., les insultes, les menaces, je n'en sais rien. C'est **une fable** – the
insults, the threats, I know nothing about them. It's all concocted.

factrice (f) – postwoman.

facture (f);
payer la facture – to foot the bill:
e.g., et qui va **payer la facture**? Nous, les contribuables – And who
is going to foot the bill? We, the taxpayers.

faste – lucky:
e.g., je suis dans un jour **faste** – I'm having a lucky day.

fauteuil roulant (m) – wheelchair.

faux;
s'inscrire en faux contre – to challenge, deny outright, dispute:
e.g., il **s'inscrit en faux contre** leur affirmation – he challenges
their claim.

fer (m);
croiser le fer avec quelqu'un – to cross swords with someone:
e.g., mon père n'hésite pas à **croiser le fer avec** le maire s'il n'est
pas content – my father doesn't hesitate to cross swords with the
mayor if he isn't pleased. (Also **ferrailler avec quelqu'un**.)

féru;
être féru de – to be very taken with:
e.g., **elle est férue** de jeux de tirage – she is into lotteries in a big
way.

feu (m);
soldats du feu – fire-fighters;
ne pas faire long feu – not to last long:
e.g., puis ils ont donné des coups de pied à la porte d'entrée qui **n'a
pas fait long feu** – then they kicked the front door which did not
last long.

feuille (f);
feuille de paye – payslip.

ficelé:
e.g., un court-métrage amusant et bien **ficelé** – an amusing and
well-constructed short film.

ficelle (f);
avec des bouts de ficelle – on a shoestring:
e.g., il faut admirer ce film fait **avec des bouts de ficelle** – one
must admire this film done on a shoestring.

fidélité (f);
carte de fidélité – loyalty card (shops, etc.).

figue (f);
mi-figue mi-raisin – neither one thing nor the other:
e.g., le temps demain sera **mi-figue mi-raisin** – the weather will be
mixed tomorrow.

fil (m);
de fil en aiguille – leading from one thing to another:
e.g., elle a parlé de son enfance et, **de fil en aiguille**, de son mariage
et de son divorce – she spoke of her childhood and, from one thing to
another, of her marriage and divorce;
être cousu de fil blanc – to be easily seen through:
e.g., leur stratégie **était cousue de fil blanc** – their strategy was
obvious.

file (f);
à la file – in a row:
e.g., trois victoires **à la file** – three wins on the trot;
stationner en double file – to double park.

filigrane (m);
en filigrane – just visible, in the background:
e.g., j'ai lu son discours qui est plein de défi mais je lis **en filigrane**
un peu d'appréhension – I have read his speech which is full of
defiance but behind it I can see a touch of apprehension.

film (m):
film gore – blood and horror film.

fin (f) **de non-recevoir** – (flat) refusal:
e.g., malgré notre optimisme ils nous ont opposé **une fin de non-
recevoir** – in spite of our optimism we met with a refusal.

fixe (m) – basic salary;
fixe intéressant – attractive salary.

flanc (m);
prêter le flanc à la critique/au ridicule – to expose oneself to
criticism/ridicule.

fléchir – to abate;
e.g., le vent **fléchit** – the wind is easing.

fliqué *:
e.g., il y a beaucoup d'ambassades ici, alors c'est un quartier très
fliqué – there are a lot of embassies here so there are cops all over
the place.

fliquer * – to watch closely, spy on:
e.g., vous êtes **fliqué**! – you are being watched!

flirt (m) – boy/girl friend:
e.g., elle boude car elle s'est fâchée avec son **flirt** – she is sulking for
she has fallen out with her boyfriend.

flottement (m) – indecision;
flottement gouvernemental – dithering by the government.

flou (m) – vagueness:
e.g., malheureusement leur proposition laisse trop de détails dans le
flou – unfortunately their proposal leaves too many details unclear.

fluide;
circulation fluide – free-flowing traffic.

foi (f);
digne de foi – trustworthy:
e.g., ce sont des gens **dignes de foi** – they are trustworthy people.

folie (f):
e.g., c'est de **la folie** douce/furieuse – it's utter madness.

fonceur (m), **fonceuse** (f) * – dynamic person, bundle of energy.

fonction (f);
appartement/voiture de fonction – flat/car that goes with the
job, is a company perk.

fond (m);
fond musical – background music;
dire/donner le fond de sa pensée – to say what one really thinks.

fontaine (f):
e.g., il ne faut pas dire '**Fontaine**, je ne boirai pas de ton eau' –
never say never.

footeux (m)/**footeuse** (f) – footie fan/player.

forçat (m) – convict;
travail de forçat – hard slog.

force (f);
la force publique – the police.

forcing (m)
faire le/du forcing – to put on (the) pressure:
e.g., Les Etats-Unis **font du forcing** en attendant une réponse
favorable – America is putting on the pressure while awaiting a
favourable answer.

fossé (m);
le fossé des générations – the generation gap.

foudres (f) – wrath, anger:
e.g., ils vont s'attirer **les foudres** de leur patron – they are going to
incur the wrath of their boss.

fouillé – thorough, in depth;
une enquête fouillée – a thorough enquiry.

fourmi (f);
un travail de fourmi – a slow arduous task.

frasque (f) – prank:
e.g., tu te rappelles **les frasques** de notre groupe? – you remember
the high jinks we lot got up to?

fraude (f) – cheating;
la fraude dans les examens – cheating in exams.

frein (m);
ronger son frein – to champ at the bit:
e.g., les paras étaient déjà là, ils **rongeaient leur frein** – the paras
were already there, raring to go.

friand;
être friand de – to have a liking for:
e.g., les Américains **sont friands de** ce genre de policier – the
Americans are keen on this kind of thriller.

frilosité (f) – (feeling of) reluctance, timidity:
e.g., **la frilosité** de beaucoup d'investisseurs en ce moment n'est
guère surprenante – the reluctance of many investors at the
moment is hardly surprising.

front (m);
faire front – to face up to things.

frontière (f):
e.g., **la frontière** est parfois mince entre l'hospitalité et la corruption
– it is sometimes a fine line between hospitality and bribery;
mais où situer **la frontière**? C'est là la question – but where do you
draw the line? That is the question.

fugue (f):
e.g., il s'agit d'une jeune fille **en fugue** – it's about a girl who has
run away.

fuite (f);
fuite des cerveaux – brain drain.

fuseau (m);
fuseau horaire – time zone.

G

gage (m) – proof:
e.g., j'ai remarqué la belle voiture devant sa porte – **le gage** de la
réussite – I noticed the nice car outside his door – evidence of how
well he had done.

gageure (f) – risky attempt:
e.g., c'est **une gageure** que de tenter de traverser à la nage – it's a
long shot trying to swim across.

galon (m);
prendre du galon – to gain promotion:
e.g., charmant et talentueux, **il prend du galon** – charming and
talented, he is moving up in the world.

gant (m);
ne pas prendre de(s) gants avec quelqu'un – to be tough on
someone, pull no punches.

garable – with room to park:
e.g., heureusement mon quartier est toujours **garable** – fortunately
you can still park around here.

garde-fou (m) – safeguard:
cette fois ils ont mis des **garde-fous** en place – this time there are
safeguards in place.

gendarme (m);
la peur du gendarme – the fear of being arrested:
e.g., 'Ce qui nous manque aujourd'hui,' ajouta le vieux, 'c'est **la peur
du gendarme**' – 'what we are missing today,' the old man added, 'is
the respect for law and order.'

genre (m);
c'est la loi du genre – that is its nature, that's the nature of the
beast:
e.g., oui, ces fausses alertes à la bombe causent beaucoup de
problèmes aux gens. **C'est la loi du genre** – yes, these false bomb
alarms cause people a lot of problems. That's the nature of them.

géométrie (f);
à géométrie variable – flexible:
e.g., la seule possibilité pour moi, c'est s'ils peuvent maintenant me composer un contrat **à géométrie variable** – the only possibility for me is if they can now work out a flexible contract (from **avion à géométrie variable** = swing-wing plane).

glas (m);
sonner le glas – to sound the death knell:
e.g., est-ce que **le glas a sonné** pour la chasse au renard en Angleterre? – is this the end of fox-hunting in England?

globalement – 1. worldwide;
                   2. in general:
e.g., j'en suis **globalement** satisfait – I'm pleased with it overall.

gommer – to erase, blot out:
e.g., il est impossible de **gommer** ces images de la guerre – it's impossible to wipe out these images of the war.

goujon (m);
taquiner le goujon * – to go fishing, enjoy some fishing.

gouvernants (m) – those who govern us.

gouverne (f):
pour votre gouverne – for your guidance.

grain (m);
veiller au grain – to keep a weather eye open:
e.g., la tension monte et je dis à mes collègues **de veiller au grain** – the tension is mounting and I tell my colleagues to be on the lookout for trouble (literally **grain** = squall in nautical language).

graine (f):
e.g., c'est de **la graine** de champion – he's a champion in the making.

grandissime – huge, great, tremendous:
e.g., notre club est **grandissime** favori pour la coupe des champions – our club is hot favourite for the champions' cup. (Some other words are similarly formed: note **brillantissime, drôlissime, gravissime, rarissime, richissime**.)

graphisme (m) – handwriting.

grassement:
e.g., il paie **grassement** tous ses employés – he pays all his employees handsomely.

grimpe (f) – rock climbing.

grincheux – grumpy, crochety.

grippe (f);
grippe aviaire – bird flu.
grippe porcine – swine flu.

grossièrement – roughly:
e.g., ça va coûter combien, **grossièrement**? – what will it cost, roughly speaking?

gruger (literary, or formal, as opposed to **escroquer**) – to swindle:
e.g., il avoue **avoir grugé** toutes ces personnes – he admits swindling all these people.

gué (m);
au milieu du gué – midstream:
e.g., il est trop tard. On ne peut pas abandonner **au milieu du gué** – It is too late. You can't give up half way (**gué** – ford).

guéguerre (f) – minor quarrel, petty spat.

guilleret – chirpy, sprightly.

gyrophare (m) – flashing light:
e.g., ils se mirent à courir en voyant **le gyrophare** d'une voiture de police – they began to run on seeing the flashing light of a police car.

H

haleine (f);
tenir en haleine – to hold captivated:
e.g., le jour de Noël beaucoup de gens ont vu ce téléfilm qui les **a tenus en haleine** – on Christmas Day a lot of people saw this TV film which held them captivated.

hallucinant – unbelievable:
e.g., le matin, après une nuit de violence, j'ai vu cette scène **hallucinante** – in the morning, after a night of violence, I saw this mind-blowing scene.

harassant – exhausting;
une journée harassante – an exhausting day.

haut;
haut et fort – loud and clear;
voir les choses de haut – to take a detached view of it all;
regarder de haut – to look down on, scorn.

hécatombe (f) – massacre.

hermétique – abstruse;
un discours hermétique – an abstruse speech.

heure (f);
heure légale – standard time (as opposed to **heure locale**);
l'heure est à la sécurité dans la capitale – security is the watchword in the capital;
à ses heures (perdues) – in one's spare time;
heures creuses – quiet, slack moments:
e.g., il y a un tarif réduit **aux heures creuses** – there is a cheap off-peak rate;
pour l'heure – for the time-being:
e.g., **pour l'heure** rien ne va changer – for the time-being there'll be no change.

heureux;
s'estimer heureux – to consider oneself lucky:
e.g., **je m'estime heureuse** d'avoir trouvé cet appartement avec un bout de jardin – I count myself lucky to have found this flat with a bit of garden.

histoire (f);
pour l'histoire – for the record.

homéopathique;
à dose(s) homéopathique(s) – in small doses:
e.g., par contre, le directeur préférait nous faire des louanges **à dose homéopathique** – on the other hand, the headmaster preferred to praise us in small doses.

homologue (m/f) – opposite number:
e.g., **mon homologue** à Paris doit me téléphoner ce soir – my opposite number in Paris is due to phone me this evening.

homonyme (m) – namesake.

hôpital (m):
e.g., c'est **l'hôpital** qui se moque de la charité – it is the pot calling the kettle black.

horion (m) (literary or jocular) – blow:
e.g., **des horions** furent échangés – blows were exchanged, there were fisticuffs.

hors champ – off camera:
e.g., cette voix **hors champ**, tu l'as reconnue? – Did you recognize that off camera voice?

hospitaliers (m) – hospital staff:
e.g., **les hospitaliers** ont réagi à la crise d'une façon très profession-nelle – the hospital staff reacted to the crisis in a very professional way.

houlette (f);
sous la houlette (de) – under the direction (of):
l'équipe est maintenant **sous la houlette d'**un nouvel entraîneur –
a new trainer is now in charge of the team.

hue:
tirer à hue et à dia – to pull in opposite directions:
e.g., il lui faudra être résolu. Malheureusement son prédécesseur **a
été tiré à hue et à dia** – He will have to be firm. Unfortunately his
predecessor was pulled one way then the other.

huile (f);
jeter/mettre de **l'huile** sur le feu – to add fuel to the flames.

huppé * – very wealthy;
les gens huppés – posh people.

hygiaphone (m) – counter grill (for customer to speak through).

hypothéquer – to put at risk, jeopardise:
e.g., cela pourrait **hypothéquer** notre projet – that could put our
project at risk.

I

idée (f);
caresser l'idée (de) – to toy with the idea (of):
e.g., **elle caresse l'idée d'**aller travailler à l'étranger – she is toying
with the idea of going to work abroad.

idoine – appropriate (rather humorous):
e.g., j'hésite devant la porte. Je dois maintenant trouver la clé **idoine**
– I hesitate outside the door. I must now find the appropriate key.

imbibé * – drunk, sozzled.

immigration (f) **clandestine** – illegal immigration.

imparable;
un alibi imparable –a cast-iron alibi.

impasse (f);
faire l'impasse sur – to opt out of, miss out:
e.g., son père est malade et elle **fait l'impasse sur** le prochain tournoi – her father is ill and she's giving the next tournament a miss.

impérativement:
e.g., votre réponse doit **impérativement** arriver avant la fin du mois – we must have your answer without fail before the end of the month.

s'imposer:
e.g., un séjour à Oxford **s'impose** – a stay in Oxford is a must.

imprenable:
e.g., une vue **imprenable** sur la baie – an unbroken view over the bay.

imprévu (m);
sauf imprévu – barring anything unforeseen.

inactif – not in work;
un ménage inactif – a household where neither person is working,

inadapté;
l'enfance inadaptée – children with special needs.

inaugurer – to open (e.g., new building):
e.g., un personnage important va sans doute **inaugurer** l'hôpital – doubtless a VIP will be opening the hospital.

incendiaire (also **pyromane**) (m/f) – arsonist.

incitation (f) – incentive;
incitations fiscales – tax incentives.

inconditionnel;
être un(e) inconditionnel(le) (de) – to be a committed fan of:
e.g., **c'est une inconditionnelle** des chansons yé-yé – she's a great fan of the '60s pop songs;
je suis un inconditionnel des fromages de Savoie – I'm a great one for the cheeses of Savoy.

incontournable – unmissable:
e.g., n'oubliez pas de visiter les salons de thé. Les pâtisseries sont **incontournables** – don't forget to visit the tea rooms. You can't miss the cakes.

indépendant;
indépendant de notre volonté – beyond our control:
e.g., nous nous excusons de ces erreurs qui étaient **indépendantes de notre volonté** –we apologise for these mistakes for which we were not responsible.

indocile – unruly, wayward (child, pupil).

indolore – painless.

informé;
jusqu'à plus ample informé (administrative) – until more is known.

ingarable – where it is impossible to park:
e.g., le weekend cette rue est **ingarable** – at the weekend you can't park anywhere in this street.

injoignable – unreachable:
e.g., il paraît qu'il est en vacances et **injoignable** – it seems he is on holiday and nobody can get hold of him.

inquiet (m), **inquiète** (f) – worrier, anxious person.

insoupçonnable – beyond suspicion.

inspiré:
e.g., il serait bien **inspiré** d'être plus poli avec son patron – he would do well to be more polite to his boss.

insubmersible – unsinkable.

intégriste (m/f) – fundamentalist.

intempéries (f) – inclement weather:
e.g., les **intempéries** d'un printemps pourri – the bad weather of a very poor spring.

intemporel – timeless.

intéresser – to affect:
e.g., ce mauvais temps va surtout **intéresser** le nord du pays – this bad weather will affect especially the north of the country.

intérimaire – temporary;
emploi intérimaire – temporary job.

interlocuteur (m), **interlocutrice** (f);
interlocuteur privilégié – important contact, link man, to have the ear of:
e.g., je suis **l'interlocuteur privilégié** du maire – I'm in close touch with the mayor.

intervention (f);
faire une intervention – 1. to make a speech;
2. to perform an operation (medical).

intimement;
être intimement convaincu – to be quite convinced.

intoxication (f) **alimentaire** – food poisoning.

irréductible – implacable, hard-line:

e.g., il fait mauvais temps dans les Alpes mais les **irréductibles** de la région ne seront pas découragés pour autant – the weather is bad in the Alps but it'll take more than that to put off the diehard fans of the region.

irrémédiable – incurable.

itinéraire (m) **bis** – alternative route.

J

jalon (m);
poser les jalons – to prepare the ground:
e.g., **ils posent les jalons** d'une solution de paix – they are preparing the ground for a peace settlement.

jardin (m)* – home patch, own backyard:
e.g., battre cette équipe quand elle joue dans son **jardin** est très difficile – beating this team on their own turf is very difficult.

jardinerie (f) – garden centre.

jeu (m);
cacher son jeu – to play one's cards close to one's chest;
calmer le jeu/les esprits – to calm things down:
e.g., **il faut calmer le jeu** avant que cette querelle ne s'envenime – we must calm things down before this quarrel gets worse;
être en jeu – to be at stake;
d'entrée de jeu – straight off, from the very beginning;
faire le jeu de quelqu'un – to play into someone's hands:
e.g., en agissant ainsi ils **font le jeu de** ces maîtres chanteurs – by acting this way they are playing into the hands of these blackmailers.

jeunisme (m) – cult of youth.

joie (f);
pour la plus grande joie de – to the delight of:
e.g., le vent a emporté mon chapeau **pour la plus grande joie des** gosses – my hat was blown off much to the kids' delight.

joignable:
e.g., elle n'est jamais **joignable**, elle est toujours en réunion – you can never contact her, she's always at a meeting.

jour (m);
sous un jour inédit – in a new light;
la vérité s'est fait jour – the truth came out;
leurs jours ne sont pas en danger – their lives are not in danger.

jucher – to perch:
e.g., **juché** sur un tabouret de bar – perched on a bar stool.

jurisprudence (f);
faire jurisprudence – to set a precedent.

juste;
voir juste – to calculate correctly:
e.g., la fourgonnette blanche des bandits venait d'arriver. Le policier sourit intérieurement. Il **avait vu juste** – the gang's white van had just arrived. The policeman smiled to himself. He had got it right.

justice (f);
se faire justice soi-même – to take the law into one's own hands.

justifier de – to prove, provide proof of:
e.g., vous aurez besoin de papiers pour **justifier de** votre indentité – you'll need papers to prove your identity.

juteux – lucrative, money-spinning;
un contrat juteux – a lucrative contract.

K

kamikaze (m/f) – suicide bomber:
e.g., **un kamikaze** s'est fait sauter au poste de contrôle – a suicide bomber blew himself up at the checkpoint.

L

la (m);
donner le la – to set the tone:
e.g., très souvent le premier match **donne le la** – very often the first match sets the tone.

lamper * – to swig:
e.g., après **avoir lampé** son vin – after knocking back his wine.

lanterne (f);
éclairer la lanterne de quelqu'un – to enlighten someone:
e.g., j'ai pu trouver l'explication que tu cherchais. C'est mon frère érudit qui **a éclairé ma lanterne** – I have managed to find the explanation you wanted. It was my learned brother who enlightened me.

larron (m);
s'entendre comme larrons en foire – to be as thick as thieves, to be hand in glove.

larvé – latent;
e.g., la crise **était larvée** depuis plusieurs mois – the crisis had been latent for several months.

légitime;
en légitime défense – in self-defence.

lest (m);
lâcher du lest – to give way, yield:
e.g., la grogne montait et le gouvernement a dû **lâcher du lest** –
the feeling of discontent was mounting, and the government had to
give ground (**lest** = ballast).

lettre (f);
avant la lettre – before one's/its time:
e.g., on peut vraiment dire que c'était un thérapeute **avant la lettre**
– one can really say that he was a therapist before his time.

lève-tôt (m/f) – early riser, early bird.

lièvre (m):
e.g., courir plusieurs **lièvres** à la fois – to pursue several things at
the same time, have a finger in more than one pie.

liquide (m) – ready cash:
e.g., je préfère payer en **liquide** – I prefer to pay cash.

lit (m);
faire le lit (de) – to prepare the ground (for):
e.g., ils **faisaient**, sans le savoir, **le lit de** l'extrémisme – they were
preparing the ground, without knowing it, for extremism.

littérature (f):
e.g., et surtout, bonne santé! Tout le reste n'est que **littérature** –
and above all, good health! Everything else counts for little.

longanimité (f) (literary) – patience, forbearance.

longiligne – tall and slim, bean pole.

longueur (f);
avoir une longueur d'avance (sur) – to have a lead (over):
e.g., il en résulte que nous **avons une longueur d'avance sur** nos
concurrents européens – the result is that we are ahead of our
European rivals.

lorgnette (f);
regarder/voir par le petit bout de la lorgnette – to have a restricted view:
e.g., il s'occupe trop des détails. Il **regarde** les choses **par le petit bout de la lorgnette** – he is too concerned with the details. He is missing the big picture. (**lorgnette** = opera glasses, but once meant telescope.)

lot (m);
se détacher/sortir du lot – to stand out from the rest.

loti;
bien/mal loti – well/badly off.

lucarne (f) – TV screen;
e.g., ce programme sera mis **en lucarne** samedi soir – this programme will be shown on Saturday night.

lumière (f);
mettre en lumière – to highlight:
e.g., ce film **a mis en lumière** les dangers du tabagisme – this film clearly revealed the dangers of smoking.

luxe (m):
e.g., un peu de politesse ne serait pas **du luxe** – we could do with a little politeness.

M

macaron (m) – badge:
e.g., il n'y avait pas de problème, peut-être à cause du **macaron** collé sur mon pare-brise – there were no problems, perhaps because of the sticker on my windscreen.

machiste – chauvinistic (also **macho**).

maille (f);
avoir maille à partir avec quelqu'un – to have a quarrel, be at odds with someone:
e.g., c'est une famille qui **a eu maille à partir avec** la justice – it's a family which has had a brush with the law.

maillon (m);
maillon faible – weak link (in the chain).

main (f);
avoir la haute main (sur) – to be in overall charge (of):
e.g., il **a la haute main sur** tous les policiers en civil ici – he has overall charge of the plain-clothes policemen here;
avoir la main heureuse – to have a lucky touch:
e.g., ils **ont eu la main heureuse** dans le choix de leur entraîneur – they picked the right one when they chose their coach;
passer la main – to hand over:
e.g., il a 70 ans mais il n'a aucune intention de **passer la main** – he is 70 but he has no intention of handing over.

maître (m);
régner en maître – to reign supreme.

majeur – of age;
ne pas être majeur – to be under age.

maldonne (f);
il y a maldonne – there's been a misunderstanding, mistake.

malentendants (m) – the hard of hearing.

malheur (m);
un malheur n'arrive/ne vient jamais seul – it never rains but it pours;
à quelque chose malheur est bon – it's an ill wind (that blows nobody any good), every cloud has a silver lining.

malin – clever, sharp, smart:
e.g., **bien malin** qui aurait pu prévoir ce résultat extraordinaire –
who could have possibly foreseen this extraordinary result.

manière (f);
recourir/avoir recours à la manière forte – to resort to strong-
arm tactics.

manteau (m);
sous le manteau – secretly:
e.g., on peut toujours les acheter **sous le manteau**, vous savez –
you can still buy them under the counter, you know.

marge (f);
marge de manoeuvre – room to manoeuvre;
ne pas avoir de marge de manoeuvre – to be boxed in.

mariée (f);
la mariée est trop belle – it's too good to be true;
se plaindre que la mariée est trop belle – to complain that you
can have too much of a good thing.

marmite (f);
faire bouillir la marmite – to keep the pot boiling:
e.g., à cette époque elle avait juste assez pour **faire bouillir la
marmite** – at that time she had just enough to keep the wolf from
the door.

marqueur (m) – felt-tip pen.

marron (m);
tirer les marrons du feu – to do a risky job for someone else's
benefit:
e.g., même si la situation dans ces pays devient dangereuse a-t-on le
droit de demander à nos troupes de **tirer les marrons du feu**? –
even if the situation in these countries becomes dangerous has one
the right to ask our troops to go in and do the risky work for them?

masse (f) **salariale** – wages' bill.

mathématique;
c'est mathématique * – it's logical:
e.g., **c'est mathématique**, vous, vous les payez bien et eux, ils travaillent bien – it follows , you pay them well, and they work well.

maugréer (contre) – to growse, gripe, chunter (about).

maximum (m);
faire le maximum – to do all one can.

méconnaître;
ne pas méconnaître que… – to be perfectly aware that…

médicalisé:
e.g., la pénurie de lits **médicalisés** – the shortage of hospital beds.

meilleur:
e.g., **les meilleures choses** ont une fin – all good things come to an end, nothing lasts for ever.

mêlée (f);
rester au-dessus de la mêlée – to stand back a bit, not to get too involved.

meubler – to fill (in):
e.g., que faites-vous pour **meubler** vos loisirs? – what do you do in your spare time?

meurtre (m) **maquillé**;
e.g., la question se pose: une mort accidentelle ou **un meurtre maquillé**? – the question is this: was it an accidental death or a murder contrived to look like one?

miette (f);
mettre en miettes – to smash to smithereens, smash up:
e.g., quelque chose – ou quelqu'un – **avait mis** son vélo **en miettes** – something – or someone – had smashed his bike to bits.

migraineux (m), **migraineuse** (f) – migraine sufferer:
e.g., ma fille est **migraineuse** aussi – my daughter also gets migraines.

mille (m);
mettre dans le mille – to hit the bull's eye:
e.g., cet homme quit attendait devant la maison avait l'air un peu louche et j'ai tout de suite téléphoné à la police. **J'ai mis dans le mille**! C'était un cambrioleur connu. – this man waiting in front of the house looked a bit shifty and I phoned the police straightaway. I was spot on! He was a known burglar.

mirador (m) – watchtower.

mire (f);
en ligne de mire – in one's sights:
e.g., cette année ils ont **en ligne de mire** la Coupe Davis – this year they have their sights on the Davis Cup.

mise (f);
être de mise – to be permissible, acceptable, appropriate:
e.g., il n'avait pas envie d'y aller mais il comprenait que c'était le Jour de Noël et que la mauvaise humeur n'**était** pas **de mise** – he didn't feel like going there but he realised it was Christmas Day and being in a bad mood was not on;
sauver la mise à quelqu'un – to rescue someone in a difficulty, get someone out of a scrape:
e.g., c'est Robert qui m'**a sauvé la mise** en me trouvant un interprète – it was Robert who saved the day by finding me an interpreter;
mise en garde – warning:
e.g., pas de **mise en garde**, rien – no warning, nothing;
mise en scène – sham (performance):
e.g., 'Le cambriolage – **mise en scène** du propriétaire?' titrait le journal local – 'The break-in – was it staged by the owner?' ran the headline of the local paper.

mitage (m) – excessive building of houses:
e.g., c'est un beau paysage. On a dû lutter contre **le mitage** – it's
lovely country. We had to fight against building on it.

mitigé – mixed:
e.g., au début j'étais assez **mitigé** – to begin with I wasn't that keen;
temps mitigé – mixed weather;
compliments mitigés – half-hearted congratulations.

mobile (m) – motive;
e.g., elle a **un mobile**, oui, mais cela ne veut pas dire qu'elle soit
coupable – she has a motive, yes, but that doesn't mean she is guilty.

moeurs (f);
faire partie des moeurs – to have become a normal part of life, to
be fully accepted:
e.g., même ici, dans cette petite île, la pause-café à 11 heures **fait
partie des moeurs** – even here, on this little island, elevenses is
an accepted part of life.

mondialisation (f) – globalisation.

monnaie (f);
rendre à quelqu'un la monnaie de sa pièce – to pay someone
back in his own coin, give someone a taste of his own medicine.

monnayer;
monnayer ses talents – to cash in on one's talents, skills.

monospace (m) – people carrier.

moral (m);
saper le moral à quelqu'un * – to knock someone for six, knock
the stuffing out of someone.

morale (f);
faire la morale à quelqu'un – to lecture someone.

motivant;
salaire motivant – attractive salary;
avantages motivants – attractive benefits.

motivation (f);
lettre de motivation – back-up letter for a job application.

mouche (f);
faire mouche – to score a bull's eye, be right on target:
e.g., ses mots d'esprit **font** toujours **mouche** – his witticisms always
strike home;
sa pénalité **fait mouche** et nous avons gagné! – his penalty is on
target and we've won!

moutonnier – sheep-like:
e.g., on peut compter sur une réaction **moutonnière** – doubtless
they will all behave like sheep.

moyennant;
moyennant rétribution – in return for payment.

multipropriété (f) – time-sharing.

musarder – to dawdle:
e.g., les automobilistes qui **musardent** sur les routes – drivers who
dawdle along.

mutation (f) – transfer (job);
demander une mutation – to request a transfer.

muter – to transfer:
e.g., elle vient d'**être mutée** à Londres – she has just been
transferred to London.

N

nager;
nager dans le bonheur – to be over the moon.

nanti – well-off;
les nantis et les non-nantis – the haves and have-nots.

nature (f);
avantages en nature – perks, benefits.

navette (f);
faire la navette – to commute, shuttle:
e.g., en bonne maman, je **fais la navette** scolaire jour après jour –
like a good mum I do the school run day after day.

nécessaire (m);
le strict nécessaire – the bare essentials.

neige (f) **fondue** – 1. sleet, 2.slush.

neutraliser – to close (to traffic):
e.g., il se peut que cette voie **soit** toujours **neutralisée** – it's
possible that lane is still closed off.

névrosé – neurotic.

noblesse (f);
acquérir ses lettres de noblesse – to gain one's credentials:
e.g., il n'y a pas de doute que les sandwicheries **ont acquis leurs
lettres de noblesse** – there is no doubt that sandwich bars are an
established success.

noir;
caisse noire – slush fund;
marée noire – oil slick (on the shore);
série noire – 1. thriller, crime story;
                2. string of misfortunes, run of bad luck:
e.g., inondations, accidents de chemin de fer, fièvre aphteuse – **la série noire** continue – floods, railway accidents, foot and mouth disease – it's one thing after another.

noir (m);
travail au noir – moonlighting.

note (f);
note de frais – expense account.

noté;
bien/mal noté – with a good/poor record:
e.g., il travaille ici depuis deux ans et il est **bien noté** – he has been working here for two years and he is well thought of.

notions (f) – basic knowledge:
e.g., il faudra aussi avoir des **notions** d'anglais – some knowledge of English would also be required.

numéraire (m) – cash.

numérique (m) – digital technology.

nue (f);
porter quelqu'un aux nues – to praise someone to the skies;
tomber des nues – to be utterly astounded.

O

obérer (literary) – to compromise, endanger:
e.g., ils **ont** déjà **obéré** leurs chances de succès – they have already compromised their chances of success.

obnubiler – to obsess;
être obnubilé par l'argent – to be obsessed by money.

obtempération (f) – obedience, compliance.

occulter – to hide, conceal:
e.g., leur propagande ne doit pas **occulter** le fait qu'ils possèdent beaucoup d'armes modernes – their propaganda mustn't obscure the fact that they have a lot of modern weaponry.

oeillères (f);
avoir des oeillères – to be blinkered:
e.g., le problème, c'est qu'ils **ont des oeillères** et ne voient pas ce qui se passe ailleurs – the trouble is that they are blinkered and don't see what is happening elsewhere.

off (m) – fringe event (at a festival);
voir quelque chose en off – to see something on the fringe.

ombre (f);
faire de l'ombre à quelqu'un – to overshadow someone.

OPA (f) – takeover bid (from **o**ffre **p**ublique d'**a**chat).

or (m);
or blanc – snow;
or noir – oil.

orée (f) – edge, verge;
à l'orée du bois – on the edge of the wood;
à l'orée de la nuit – on the brink of darkness.

orfèvre (m);
être orfèvre en la matière – to be an expert:
e.g., je m'adresse à lui parce qu'il **est orfèvre en la matière** – I
turn to him because he knows all about such things.

ovalie (f) – rugby (football) world.

oxygène (m);
être un ballon d'oxygène – to be a lifesaver:
e.g., ses visites quotidiennes **ont été** pour moi **un vrai ballon
d'oxygène** – her daily visits were what really kept me going.

P

pactiser;
pactiser avec quelqu'un – to come to terms with someone:
e.g., **pactiser avec** les rebelles est impensable – to make a deal
with the rebels is unthinkable.

pactole (m) – riches, fortune:
e.g., c'est **un** joli **pactole** comparé à mon salaire d'autrefois – it's a
nice sum compared with what I was earning before.

page (f):
e.g., elle veut maintenant **tourner la page** – she wants now to
move on.

pain (m):
e.g., **manger son pain blanc** le premier – to have it easy to begin
with., have jam today.

palme (f);
remporter la palme – to be the winner, carry off the prize, come
out on top.

palmarès (m);
avoir à son palmarès – to have to one's credit.

paniquant – scary.

panne (f);
panne d'oreiller * – oversleeping:
e.g., **une panne d'oreiller** n'est pas une excuse, m'a-t-on dit –
oversleeping is no excuse, I was told.

papoter * – to chat, gossip, natter.

parc (m) **naturel** – nature reserve.

parcours (m);
accident/incident de parcours – mishap, hiccup:
e.g., oui, les chiffres de vente sont décevants mais ce n'est qu'**un**
accident de parcours – yes, the sales figures are disappointing
but it's just a blip.

parent (m);
parent pauvre – poor relation:
e.g., ni le gouvernement ni la presse ne font beaucoup pour
promouvoir notre sport. Nous sommes un peu **le parent pauvre** –
neither the government nor the press is doing much to promote our
sport. We are something of the poor relation.

parenthèse (f);
mettre entre parenthèses – to put to one side:
e.g., pour l'instant ce souci **est mis entre parenthèses** – for the
moment this worry is put to one side.

parer;
parer au plus pressé – to see to first things first:
e.g., ma mère est habituée à **parer au plus pressé** – my mother is
used to dealing with the most important things first.

parfum (m);
être le parfum du jour * – to be the flavour of the month.

pari (m);
tous les paris sont ouverts – it's anyone's guess, it's wide open.

partage (m);
le partage de l'emploi/du travail – job sharing.

participation (f) – contribution, payment:
e.g., on vous demandera aussi **une petite participation** – you'll
also be asked for a small payment.

partie (f);
avoir la partie belle – to be nicely placed, on to a good thing;
faire partie intégrante de – to be an essential part of.

pas (m);
pas de tir – launch pad (space rockets);
se mettre au pas – to toe the line;
sortir/tirer quelqu'un d'un mauvais pas – to get someone out of
a mess;
emboîter le pas à quelqu'un – to fall into step with someone:
e.g., La France et l'Italie ont accepté et les autres pays vont sans
doute leur **emboîter le pas** – France and Italy have accepted and
the other countries will doubtless follow suit.

pâté (m) – block (of houses);
faire le tour du pâté de maisons – to go round the block.

pavé (m);
tenir le haut du pavé – to enjoy high status:
e.g., ce dimanche à la télé les finales de Wimbledon **tiennent le haut
du pavé** – this Sunday on TV the Wimbledon finals have the place
of honour;
pavé dans la mare – commotion, big shock:
e.g., cette accusation est **un pavé dans la mare** du ministre – this
accusation is a bombshell for the minister;
c'est le pavé de l'ours – (said when good intentions only make
matters worse; this and the previous expression are both from La
Fontaine – the first one is commonly used);
un gros pavé * – a hefty tome, bulky volume.

paysage (m) **politique** – political landscape.

peaufiner – to polish, perfect, touch up.

pêcheur (m);
les pêcheurs à la ligne * – stay-away voters (preferring to cast a line rather than a vote; one imagines them having gone fishing).

pécule (m) – savings;
arrondir son maigre pécule – to top up one's modest savings.

peine (f);
ne pas marchander sa peine – not to spare one's efforts.

pépinière (f) – nursery, breeding ground:
e.g., c'est **une pépinière** de jeunes rebelles – it's a breeding ground for young rebels.

perche (f);
tendre la perche – to extend a helping hand, reach out.

perdurer – to endure:
e.g., c'est une bonne vieille tradition qui **perdure** – it's a good old tradition which carries on.

perfusion (f) – drip (medical);
être sous perfusion – to be on a drip.

péricliter – to collapse:
e.g., une économie qui **périclite** – an economy on the verge of collapse.

périscolaire – extra curricular.

permettre;
comme ce/il n'est pas permis * – utterly, wildly, impossibly (the expression is used as an intensifier):
e.g., soudain aujourd'hui elle se sent heureuse **comme il n'est pas permis** – suddenly today she is feeling unbelievably happy.

persister et signer * – to stick to one's story, not to budge (the expression is an amusing reference to someone making a statement to the police) :
e.g., son discours était amusant – et eurosceptique. Il **persiste et signe** – his speech was amusing – and Eurosceptical. He is sticking to his guns;
le mauvais temps **persiste et signe** – there is no sign of the bad weather changing.

perso *;
jouer perso – to be selfish, go one's own selfish way. Also used in a sporting context, typically of a player who hogs the ball (from **personnel**).

perte (f);
courir à sa perte – to be heading for disaster.

pertinemment;
savoir pertinemment que … – to know perfectly well that …

petit-déjeuner – to breakfast.

pétri;
être pétri de talent – to be full of talent.

phare (m);
c'était une des équipes **phare** des années 80 – it was one of the standout teams of the '80s.

phase (f);
être en phase (avec) – to be in touch (with):
e.g., le ministre dit toujours qu'il **est en phase avec** les étudiants – the minister is always saying he is in tune with students.

photomaton (m) – (take-your-own-picture) photo booth.

phrase (f);
petite phrase – soundbite:
e.g., chez nous elle est surtout connue pour ses **petites phrases** –
with us she is especially known for her soundbites.

pièce (f);
**créer/fabriquer/inventer/monter/ quelque chose de toutes
pièces** – to make something up from beginning to end:
e.g., selon moi sa version des faits **est fabriquée de toutes pièces**
– in my opinion her version of events is made up from beginning to
end.

pied (m);
au pied levé – straight off:
e.g., il est difficile de remplacer un collègue **au pied levé** – it is
difficult to cover for a colleague just like that;
lâcher pied – to give ground:
e.g., il semble que le ministère **lâche pied** peu à peu – it seems that
the ministry is gradually giving ground;
mettre quelqu'un à pied – to dismiss, fire someone;
ne pas savoir sur quel pied danser – to be at one's wits' end, not
to know which way to turn.

piégé;
un attentat suicide à la voiture piégée – a suicide car-bomb
attack.

pierre (f);
vieilles pierres – old buildings:
e.g., leur passion, c'est **les vieilles pierres** – their great interest is
in old buildings;
jour à marquer d'une pierre blanche – red letter day;
pierre angulaire – cornerstone:
e.g., c'est **la pierre angulaire** de leur foi – it is the cornerstone of
their faith;
pierre d'achoppement – stumbling block;
apporter sa pierre à quelque chose – to make one's contribution
towards something:
e.g., je veux **apporter**, moi aussi, **ma pierre** à ce debat – I too want
to contribute to this discussion.

piétonne (f) – pedestrian precinct (for **rue piétonne**).

pingouin (m);
l'habit de pingouin * – tails

pion (m);
damer le pion à quelqu'un – to outmanoeuvre, stymie someone:
e.g., elle m'**a damé le pion** en changeant son numéro de téléphone –
she outsmarted me by changing her phone number.

pirate (m) – hacker (computers).

piscinable – where you could put a swimming pool, suitable for a
swimming pool (a useful word in property advertisements).

place (f);
dans la place – on the inside:
e.g., si vous avez des amis **dans la place**, tant mieux – if you have
friends on the inside, so much the better (**place** in its meaning of
fortress).

plafond (m);
crever le plafond – to go through the roof (prices).

plancher sur – to work on:
e.g., ils **planchent** toujours **sur** cette question épineuse – they are
still working on this tricky question.

planétaire – worldwide;
succès planétaire – worldwide success.

planifier – to plan:
e.g., je commence à **planifier** mon séjour en Australie – I'm
beginning to plan my stay in Australia.

plasticien (m), **plasticienne** (f) – plastic surgeon (for **chirurgien
plasticien**).

plastiquer – to blow up:
e.g., deux bâtiments **ont été plastiqués** ce matin – there were
bomb attacks on two buildings this morning.

plat;
remettre quelque chose à plat – to go back to the drawing board,
start all over again.

plateau-télé (m) – TV supper.

plate-forme (f) (aéroportuaire) – airport:
e.g., on parle même d'une deuxième **plate-forme** puisque la région
reçoit de plus en plus de visiteurs – there is even talk of a second
airport since the region is getting more and more visitors.

plébisciter – to show wide support for:
e.g., les Anglais **plébiscitent** le beaujolais nouveau – the new
beaujolais goes down well with the English.

plus;
sans plus – no more:
e.g., un repas acceptable, **sans plus** – an acceptable meal, no more
than that.

les **PME** (f) – small businesses (from **petites et moyennes
entreprises**), SMEs.

poids (m);
avoir deux poids (et) deux mesures – to have double standards.

point (m);
être au point mort – to be at a standstill:
e.g., les pourparlers **sont au point mort** – the talks have stalled.

pointe (f);
à la pointe de la technique – at the cutting edge of technology.

pointer – to clock on, sign on:
pointer au chômage – to sign on the dole:
e.g., il doit **pointer** dans un commissariat une fois par semaine – he
has to report to a police station once a week.

pointillé;
en pointillé – on and off:
e.g., mon projet demeure **en pointillé** – my project makes on and off progress.

poire (f);
entre la poire et le fromage – towards the end of a good meal:
e.g., c'est une confidence qu'elle m'a faite **entre la poire et le fromage** – it is something she confided in me over a good meal.

poisson (m);
noyer le poisson – to be evasive, duck the question, stall.

polyvalence (f) – versatility, all-round skills:
e.g., j'admire **la polyvalence** de ces jeunes acteurs – I admire the versatility of these young actors.

pont (m);
un pont d'or – a golden hello.

portable (m) – mobile (phone); **le mobile** is also used.

porte-à-faux (m);
mettre quelqu'un en porte-à-faux – to put someone in a tricky situation:
e.g., on en rit mais cet épisode **met** le gouvernement **en porte-à-faux** – people laugh about it but this episode puts the government in a tricky position.

poseur (m), **poseuse** (f) **de bombes** – bomber (person).

posologie (f) – dosage instructions (medicine).

possédants (m) – the rich, those who have got it all.

posté;
personnel posté – shift workers.

postuler (à) – to apply for (a job):
e.g., franchement, si j'avais su, je n'aurais pas **postulé** – frankly, if I had known, I would not have put in for the job.

pot (m);
recoller les pots cassés* – to patch things up.

poubelle (f);
télé-poubelle – rubbish TV.

pouce (m);
donner un coup de pouce – to give a bit of help, help along.

se pourlécher – to lick one's lips (in anticipation):
e.g., **je me pourlèche** de ce voyage – I can't wait for this trip.

pourquoi (m);
le pourquoi et le comment – the why and the wherefore;
le pourquoi de son licenciement – the reason for his dismissal.

précaire;
travail précaire – short-term job (with no long-term security).

précocement – early:
e.g., heureusement on a repéré les signes **précocement** et elle s'en
est complètement remise – fortunately the signs were spotted early
on and she made a complete recovery.

préfigurer – to foreshadow.

prélèvement (m);
prélèvement automatique – direct debit/standing order.

près:
e.g., elle n'est pas **près** de retourner à ce restaurant – she is not
likely to go back to that restaurant.

présage (m) – omen;
un bon présage – a good omen.

présager;
cela ne **présage** rien de bon – that sounds ominous, I don't like the
sound of that.

prescripteur (m), **prescripteuse** (f) – consultant (medical – for **médecin prescripteur**).

présélectionner – to shortlist.

présent;
répondre présent – to answer the call, be there when needed: e.g., j'essaie de **répondre présent** quand mes anciens élèves ont besoin de moi – I try to be available when an ex-pupil needs me (the image of the roll call).

presse (f) **people**. People here are not just any people but specifically well-known people. **Les people** means **les gens connus**. Thus **la presse people** refers to the publications such as magazines which focus on celebrities and their doings.

prêt;
être fin prêt – to be all set.

prévaloir – to prevail:
e.g., heureusement le bon sens **a prévalu** – fortunately common sense prevailed.

prévisible – predictable.

prime (f);
en prime – on top, in addition, for good measure, as a bonus: e.g., le barman dit qu'il fera très froid demain avec des flocons de neige **en prime** – the bartender says it'll be very cold tomorrow with some snowflakes thrown in.

primo-accédant (m), **primo-accédante** (f) – first time home-buyer.

prise (f);
être en prise directe (avec) – to be in close touch (with):
e.g., leur gouvernement **est en prise directe avec** les problèmes des sans-emploi – their government is closely concerned with the problems of the unemployed.

privatif – private:
e.g., derrière les appartements il y a un jardin **privatif** – behind the flats there is a private garden.

privilégier – to favour:
e.g., pour le moment la police ne **privilégie** pas l'hypothèse du chantage – for the moment the police do not think it's blackmail.

procès (m);
faire un procès d'intention (à quelqu'un) – to make a false accusation, put words into someone's mouth, misrepresent.

prodige (m);
faire des prodiges – to work wonders;
cela tient du prodige – it borders on the miraculous, it's quite amazing.

profit (m);
passer quelque chose par profits et pertes – to write something off.

programme (m);
ne pas être prévu au programme – not to be expected, not what was meant to happen:
e.g., ils étaient sur le point d'ouvrir le coffre-fort lorsque le veilleur de nuit a décidé de sortir fumer une cigarette, ce qui **n'était pas prévu au programme** – they were about to open the safe when the nightwatchman decided to go outside for a smoke, which was not in the script.

prolongé;
weekend prolongé – long week-end.

prompteur (m) – autocue.

pronostiquer – to forecast:
e.g., le résultat de ce match est difficile à **pronostiquer** – it's hard to forecast the result of this match.

propos (m) – words, comments, talk;
propos racistes – racist remarks.

proximité (f);
magasins de proximité – local shops.

punaiser – to pin up:
e.g., elle regardait la photo **punaisée** au mur – she was looking at
the photo pinned up on the wall (**punaise** = drawing pin).

purger;
purger sa peine – to serve one's sentence.

Q

qualité (f) – status:
e.g., on voulait savoir où j'allais, où je demeurais, ma **qualité** et ainsi
de suite – they wanted to know where I was going, where I lived, my
profession and so on.;
en ma qualité de diplomate – in my position as a diplomat.

quart de tour (m);
au quart de tour * – straight off, promptly:
e.g., encore mieux, il répond à nos plaintes **au quart de tour** –
better still, he answers our complaints very quickly (the basic image
of cranking up a car).

R

rabais (m);
au rabais – on the cheap:
e.g., il a tenté de recruter **au rabais** et ses problèmes ont bientôt
commencé – he tried to recruit on the cheap and his problems soon
began.

se rabattre sur – to fall back on:
e.g., le restaurant était fermé et nous avons dû **nous rabattre sur** le petit café – the restaurant was closed and we had to fall back on the little café.

racketter quelqu'un – to extract money from someone:
e.g., il **a racketté** quelques élèves plus jeunes qui n'osaient rien dire – he got money out of some younger pupils who didn't dare say anything.

se radicaliser – to harden:
e.g., leur position **se radicalise** – they are hardening their position.

raison (f);
s'en faire une raison – to accept the situation, make the best of it.

ralentisseur (m) – traffic-calming hump.

rallonge (f) – extra payment:
e.g., **une rallonge** est toutefois possible avant Noël – some extra money is however possible before Christmas.

ramassage (m);
car de ramassage – school bus (which picks up pupils).

se ramener à – to come down to:
e.g., ses explications **se ramènent** presque **à** un aveu – his explanations almost come down to a confession.

ras;
rempli à ras bord – 1. filled to the brim (glass, etc.);
2. chock-a-block.

ratisser;
ratisser large – to search far and wide:
e.g., les chasseurs de tête savent **ratisser large** – headhunters know how to cast the net wide.

ravaler – 1. to clean (up):
e.g., la façade **a été ravalée** – the front of the building has been cleaned;
　　　　　2. to stifle;
ravaler ses craintes – to stifle one's fears.

razzier – to plunder:
e.g., des gosses **ont razzié** notre verger – kids have plundered our orchard.

réactualiser – to update.

réalisable – feasible.

rechange (m);
une politique de rechange – an alternative policy, plan B.

récidiver – 1. to reoffend (crime);
　　　　　　2. to do it again:
e.g., elle a gagné ce tournoi en 1999 et **a récidivé** deux ans plus tard – she won this tournament in 1999 and repeated the performance two years later.

recouper – to cross-check.

recul (m);
avec du/le recul – with hindsight.

reculade (f) – climb-down.

reculé;
en des temps reculés – in distant days.

reddition (f) – surrender (military also general).

redevable;
être redevable à – to be indebted to:
e.g., encore une fois nous **sommes redevables à** nos services d'urgence – once again we are indebted to our emergency services.

rédhibitoire;
des prix rédhibitoires – prohibitive prices.

rediffusion (f) – repeat:
e.g., à Noël il y a toujours beaucoup de **rediffusions** – at Christmas there are always a lot of repeats.

réel;
balles réelles – live bullets.

réfléchir:
e.g., en attendant, ils ont demandé à **réfléchir** – meanwhile they want to think it over.

réflexion (f) – debate, discussion:
e.g., **une réflexion** sur le problème du logement aura bientôt lieu, nous a-t-on promis – there will be a debate on the housing problem soon, they've promised;
délai de réflexion – cooling-off period, time to think things over;
groupe de réflexion – think-tank.

refouler – to turn back:
e.g., ils **ont été refoulés** par la police frontalière – they have been turned back by the border police.

régresser:
e.g., la criminalité **régresse** – crime is down.

régulier;
être en situation régulière – to have one's papers in order, have the proper documents (as opposed to **en situation irrégulière**).

réhabiliter – to restore:
e.g., depuis, comme tu vois, tous ces bâtiments **ont été réhabilités** – since then, as you can see, all these buildings have been restored.

réinsertion (f) – rehabilitation;
centre de réinsertion – rehabilitation centre.

relais (m);
passer le relais à quelqu'un – to hand over (e.g. business) to someone. (The image of the relay race.)

relativiser:
e.g., il faut **relativiser** l'affaire – the matter must be put in perspective.

remaniement (m) – reorganisation;
remaniement ministériel – cabinet reshuffle.

remise (f) – remission;
remise de peine – reduction of (prison) sentence.

rentabiliser – to make profitable:
e.g., j'espère toutefois **rentabiliser** ma période de convalescence – I'm hoping, however, to make good use of my convalescence.

rentable – profitable:
e.g., il espère que son invention sera **rentable** – he hopes his invention will bring in money.

répercuter – to pass on (cost):
e.g., nous serons obligés de **répercuter** la hausse sur nos clients – we shall have to pass on the increase to our customers.

repère (m) – landmark;
prendre ses repères – to get one's bearings.

réplique (f) – aftershock (earthquake):
e.g., **la réplique** a fait courir tout le monde – the aftershock sent everyone running.

résilier;
résilier un contrat – to cancel a contract.

se ressourcer – to recharge one's batteries, refresh oneself.

restreint – restricted;
offre restreinte – limited offer.

résultat (m);
(le) résultat des courses * − the outcome (the expression is from horse racing):
e.g., **résultat des courses**, on a raté le train − the upshot was we missed the train.

retenir − to accept:
e.g., son manuscrit n'**a** pas **été retenu** − his manuscript was not accepted;
ils étaient très gentils mais je n'**ai** pas **été retenue** − they were very nice but I didn't get the job.

retirer − to pick up, collect (e.g., tickets, luggage):
e.g., il faut **retirer** les billets avant midi − we must pick up the tickets before midday.

rétorsion (f) − retaliation:
e.g., des mesures de **rétorsion** ne sont pas exclues − retaliatory measures cannot be ruled out.

rétrograder (quelqu'un) − to demote, downgrade.

réunir − to raise, collect together:
e.g., elle a réussi à **réunir** une somme importante − she managed to raise a large sum.

rêve (m);
dans ses **rêves** les plus fous − in one's wildest dreams.

revendiquer − to claim responsibility for, admit to:
e.g., jusqu'ici personne n'**a revendiqué** cette atrocité − so far no one has claimed responsibility for this atrocity.

revers (m);
balayer d'un revers de main − to wave aside:
e.g., le ministre des Affaires étrangères **a balayé** ces critiques **d'un revers de main** − the Foreign Secretary waved aside these criticisms.

révolu − past:
e.g., cette époque **est révolue** − those days are over.

rideau (m) **de fer** – metal shutter (shops).

ristourne (f) – discount;
bénéficier d'une ristourne – to get a discount.

RMiste (m/f) – someone on low-income support (from **le revenu minimum d'insertion**).

robot (m) – food processor (for **robot ménager**).

rodéo (m) – joyriding:
e.g., avant on ne pouvait guère dormir la nuit à cause des **rodéos** – before, you could hardly sleep at night because of the joyriding.

roi (m);
le roi n'est pas son cousin – he is as pleased as Punch:
e.g., il roule en Rolls, **le roi n'est pas son cousin** – he drives along in a Rolls, feeling very pleased with himself.

rompre – to break up, split up:
e.g., David et Louise viennent de **rompre** – David and Louise have just broken up.

rouler;
rouler pour quelqu'un – to back, support, be behind someone.

route (f);
tenir la route – to be solid, reliable, to hold up:
e.g., c'est un romancier dont les livres **tiennent** toujours **la route** – he's a novelist whose books always stand up well;
ces excuses ne **tiennent** pas **la route** – these excuses don't hold up.

rue (f);
être à la rue – to be on the streets, down and out.

rupestre;
l'art rupestre – cave paintings.

rupture (f);
être en rupture de stock – to be out of stock, out of it/them.

S

sabot (m) – clamping:
e.g., attention! Si vous stationnez là, vous risquez **un sabot** – Watch out! If you park there you could get clamped.

sabrer – to slash;
sabrer dans les effectifs – to make drastic cuts in the workforce.

sac (m);
sac poubelle – bin bag, black bag;
être pris la main dans le sac – to be caught with one's hand in the till, in the act.

saccage (m) – vandalism:
e.g., en première page j'ai lu '**saccage** de voyous dans le jardin public' – on the front page I read 'yobs vandalise the public gardens'.

sainteté (f):
e.g., ne pas être en odeur de **sainteté** auprès de quelqu'un – not to be in somebody's good books.

saisonnier (m), **saisonnière** (f) – seasonal worker.

salaire (m);
salaire de départ – starting salary;
les bas salaires – low earners.

salut (m);
planche de salut – last hope:
e.g., on me dit que c'est notre dernière **planche de salut** mais j'ai refusé de payer la rançon – they say it's our last hope but I have refused to pay the ransom.

sanguin;
test sanguin – blood test.

sanitaire;
avion sanitaire – air ambulance.

sans-grade (m/f);
les sans-grade – those of lower rank, the nobodies.

sans-papiers (m/f) – illegal immigrant.

santé (f);
se refaire une santé – to recover, get back to good form:
e.g., **se refaire une santé** au bord de la mer – to recuperate by the sea.

sape (f);
travail de sape – gradual undermining (e.g. of authority).

sarabande (f) – din:
e.g., **la sarabande** de la pluie sur le toit – the racket of the rain on the roof.

saturer – to saturate, swamp:
e.g., à cause de la panique le standard est **saturé** – because of the panic the switchboard is jammed.;
l'autoroute est **saturée** – the motorway is heavily congested.

schématiser – to oversimplify.

scotcher – to stick (with Sellotape):
e.g., je remarquai qu'elle **avait scotché** un numéro de téléphone au volant – I noticed she had sellotaped a phone number to the steering wheel.

S D F (m/f) – homeless person (from <u>s</u>ans <u>d</u>omicile <u>f</u>ixe).

secousse (f);
secousse tellurique/sismique – earth tremor.

sellette (f);
être sur la sellette – to be in the hot seat:
e.g., cette fois les banques **sont sur la sellette** – this time banks are under scrutiny.

semonce (f) – warning shot (across the bows):
e.g., il n'y a pas de doute que ceci représente **un coup de semonce**
pour la direction – there is no doubt that this represents a warning
shot for management.

sensation (f);
les amateurs de sensations fortes – thrill seekers, adrenalin
addicts.

séquelles (f) – after-effects:
e.g., elle gardera longtemps les **séquelles** – the after-effects will be
with her for a long time.

sérail (m);
un homme du sérail – a man close to the leader, part of the inner
set (e.g., in politics).

série (f);
tueur en série – serial killer;
la loi des séries – these things happen one after the other:
e.g., trois incendies importants en centre-ville en trois semaines, c'est
la loi des séries – three serious fires in the town centre in three
weeks, calamity follows calamity.

sérieux (m);
ne pas garder/tenir son sérieux – not to keep a straight face.

serpent (m);
serpent de mer – unimportant piece of old news (to make up for a
lack of real news), old chestnut:
e.g., 'qu'est-ce que tu lis dans le journal?' 'L'histoire de nos châteaux
hantés.' 'Ah! ce vieux **serpent de mer**!' – 'what are you reading in
the paper?' 'The story of our haunted castles.' 'Ah! that old story!'

simple;
pourquoi faire simple (quand on peut faire compliqué?) –
there's nothing like being complicated! (humorous/ironic; the last
part is sometimes left unsaid).

simulacre (m);
un simulacre d'exécution – a mock execution.

social;
dialogue social – talks between management and unions;
paix sociale – industrial peace.

soignant;
personnel soignant – medical staff.

soin (m);
être aux petits soins pour quelqu'un – to take every care of, fuss over, coddle someone.

soldate (f) – woman soldier.

soleil (m);
faire un soleil – to somersault:
e.g., selon un témoin oculaire la voiture **a fait un soleil** – according to an eye-witness the car did a somersault.

sophologie (f) – relaxation therapy.

soudoyer – to bribe.

sourdine (f);
mettre une sourdine – to tone down:
e.g., rien n'indique qu'ils vont **mettre une sourdine** à leurs plaintes – there is no sign that they are going to moderate their complaints.

sous-effectif (m);
e.g., nous tournons en **sous-effectif** – we are short-staffed.

soutien (m);
soutien moral – moral support;
cours de soutien – remedial, backup lessons.

spot (m) – (television) commercial:
e.g., quelle est l'influence des **spots** télévisés? – what influence do TV ads have?

SRAS (m) – SARS (from <u>s</u>yndrome <u>r</u>espiratoire <u>a</u>igu <u>s</u>évère).

stressant – stressful.

subjuguant – captivating:
e.g., une vue **subjuguante** – a spellbinding view.

subodorer – to suspect:
e.g., j'**ai subodoré** quelque chose de louche – I suspected something a bit iffy.

suivre:
e.g., les enfants qui ne **suivent** pas à l'école – children who can't keep up at school.

sujet (m);
sortir du sujet – to get off the point.

summum (m);
le summum de l'hypocrisie – the height of hypocrisy.

superflu (m) – extras:
e.g., j'ai fait de mon mieux pour lui donner un peu de **superflu** – I've done my best to give her a few little luxuries.

suraccident (m) – big accident, huge pile-up:
e.g., on parle d'un **suraccident** sur l'autoroute – there is talk of a big pile-up on the motorway.

surcharge (f) – overloading;
le surcharge des classes – overcrowded classes.

surclasser – 1. to outclass;
              2. to upgrade:
e.g., on m'**avait surclassée** et une bouteille de champagne m'attendait! – I had been upgraded and a bottle of champagne was awaiting me!

surenchère (f) – outbidding, outdoing, going one better;
surenchère politique – political one-upmanship, point scoring.

surestimer – to overrate:
e.g., un roman **surestimé** – an overrated novel.

surmédiatisation (f) – over-the-top media coverage.

surménage (m) – (mental) overwork, overdoing it.

surplace (m);
faire du surplace – to mark time, inch forward:
e.g., je ne vois qu'une file de voitures qui **font du surplace** – all I
can see is a queue of cars stuck in a jam;
les discussions **font du surplace** – the talks are going nowhere
fast.

surpoids (m) – being over-weight.

surprise (f);
sans surprise – straightforward, without a catch:
e.g., c'est un prix forfaitaire, **sans surprise**, comme il m'a dit plus
d'une fois – it's an all-in price with no hidden extras, as he told me
more than once.

surréaction (f) – overreaction.

sursis (m);
une peine avec sursis – a suspended sentence (legal).

T

table (f);
s'asseoir à la table des grands – to sit at high table, be up with
the big boys;
table ronde – conference, discussion group:
e.g., il a promis d'organiser **une table ronde** pour le débattre – he
has promised to arrange a conference to discuss it.

tableau (m);
pour compléter le tableau – on top of everything else:
e.g., **pour compléter le tableau** ma fille avait perdu le billet
gagnant – to crown it all my daughter had lost the winning ticket;
noircir le tableau – to paint a black picture.

tambour (m);
tambour battant – energetically and vigorously:
e.g., le nouveau directeur a introduit ces nouvelles méthodes
tambour battant – the new headmaster rapidly set about bringing
in these new methods.

tangent;
cas tangent – borderline case.

tapis (m);
tapis vert – conference table;
autour du tapis vert – around the conference table (**tapis** in its
meaning of cloth, baize).

tarauder – to pester, bug, torment:
e.g., j'**ai été** longtemps **taraudé** par cette pensée – for a long time I
was tormented by this thought.

taxi (m), **femme** (f) **taxi** – taxi driver:
e.g., c'est comment, la vie d'un **taxi**? – what's it like being a taxi
driver?

témoin (m);
passer le témoin à quelqu'un – to hand over to someone (e.g.,
business). (**témoin** = relay baton.)

temps (m);
par les temps qui courent – nowadays;
en temps et lieu/en heure – in due course;
le temps presse – time is short.

tendre;
ne pas être tendre avec/pour quelqu'un – not to treat someone kindly:
e.g., naturellement ces fonctionnaires **ne sont pas tendres avec** ceux qui discutent le bout de gras – naturally these officials don't go easy on those who argue the toss.

terme (m);
à terme – ultimately;
e.g., **à terme** tout cela va complètement changer – in the long run all that will change completely.

terrain (m):
e.g., le nouveau patron est un homme de **terrain**. Cela change tout – the new boss is a man of practical experience, he has been there and done it. That changes everything.

terreau (m) – compost:
e.g., les jeunes marginaux sont **un terreau** fertile pour les mouvements de protestation – young people on the fringe are fertile ground for protest movements.

tétaniser;
être tétanisé par la peur – to be petrified, scared rigid.

tête (f);
sur un coup de tête – on the spur of the moment.

thébaïde (f) (literary) – secluded retreat:
e.g., il a retrouvé **sa thébaïde** en Provence pour écrire un livre – he is back in his solitary hideaway in Provence in order to write a book.

thésauriser – to hoard (money):
e.g., mon fils ne veut rien dépenser, il préfère **thésauriser** son argent de poche – my son won't spend anything, he prefers to hoard his pocket money.

ticket (m);
ticket à gratter – scratch card.

tirer;
prix tirés – slashed prices;
tirer sur quelqu'un – to criticise someone:
e.g., ne **tirez** pas **sur** les professeurs – don't knock the teachers.

titiller – to tease, josh:
e.g., on **l'a titillé** un peu à cause de son accent – he came in for a bit of ribbing because of his accent.

toboggan (m) **d'évacuation** – escape chute (aeroplanes).

tocsin (m);
sonner le tocsin – to sound the alarm.

tollé (m);
provoquer un tollé – to cause an outcry.

top (m);
donner le top – to give the go-ahead:
e.g., le pilote attend **le top** – the pilot is waiting for the off.

toquer;
toquer à la porte – to knock, rap on the door.

torchon (m):
e.g., **le torchon brûle** entre ces deux voisins – there is a row going on between these two neighbours.

touche (f);
sur la touche – on the sidelines:
e.g., le monde du high-tech leur fait peur et les laisse de plus en plus **sur la touche** – the world of high-tech frightens them and leaves them increasingly on the sidelines.

à touche-touche – very close together:
e.g., le matin toutes les voitures sont **à touche-touche** – in the mornings all the cars are bumper to bumper;
les candidats sont **à touche-touche** – the candidates are almost neck and neck.

tour (m);
plus souvent qu'à son tour – all too often:
e.g., elle arrive en retard **plus souvent qu'à son tour**– she arrives late all too often.

tourner;
tourner la loi – to get round the law.

tourniquet (m) – 1. tourniquet;
2. turnstile;
3. revolving door;
4. revolving stand (for postcards).

tournis (m) * – giddiness.

tout-venant (m) – everyday stuff, nothing special:
e.g., parmi **le tout-venant** on peut parfois trouver une bonne affaire – among the usual stuff you can sometimes find a good bargain.

tractations (f) – dealings, discussions:
e.g., après de longues **tractations** téléphoniques – after lengthy discussions on the phone.

train (m);
mener grand train – to enjoy the high life, spend as if there was no tomorrow.

traîne (f);
rester à la traîne – to lag behind:
e.g., pour le moment l'Angleterre **reste à la traîne** par manque de fonds – for the moment England lags behind for lack of funds.

trait (m);
tirer un trait sur quelque chose – to draw a line under something, put in the past:
e.g., elle espère maintenant **tirer un trait sur** cet événement pénible – she hopes now to draw a line under this painful episode.

trancher – to make a decision:

e.g., le Premier ministre doit **trancher** sans délai – the Prime Minister must decide without delay;

trancher avec – to be very different from:

e.g., il faut dire que sa direction **tranche avec** celle de son prédécesseur – one has to say that his management is very different from that of his predecessor.

tranquillité (f);
tranquillité d'esprit – peace of mind.

trappe (f);
passer à la trappe – to be pushed out, vanish from sight, be discarded:

e.g., un ministre **est** encore **passé à la trappe** – another minister has gone.

travers (m);
passer au travers – to get away with it, escape:

e.g., les dangers de la jungle sont connus mais heureusement je **suis passé au travers** – the dangers of the jungle are well known but luckily I got away with it.

trésorerie (f);
problèmes de trésorerie – cashflow problems.

tribut (m);
payer un lourd tribut – to pay a heavy price:

e.g., ils ont gagné, oui. Mais quels sacrifices! Ils **ont payé un lourd tribut** – they won, yes. But what sacrifices! They paid a heavy price.

triomphe (m);
avoir le triomphe modeste – to be modest in success.

triple (m);
triple idiot – complete idiot, utter fool.

trombe (f) d'eau – cloudburst.

tronc (m);
homme tronc – talking head, presenter (TV);
tronc commun – core syllabus.

trou (m);
trou de mémoire – lapse of memory.

troupe (f);
envoyer la troupe – to send in the army.

truquer – to fake;
truquer les comptes – to fiddle the books.

tunnel (m);
voir le bout/la sortie du tunnel – to see light at the end of the tunnel.

tutoyer;
tutoyer * la perfection – to be close to perfection.

U

ultérieurement – later:
e.g., merci de rappeler **ultérieurement** – please call back later (telephone).

unique;
parent unique – single parent.

universitaire (m/f) – academic.

urgences (f);
aller aux urgences – to go to casualty, A & E.

urgentiste (m/f) – emergency doctor.

urnes (f);
aller aux urnes – to go to the polls:
e.g., le verdict des **urnes** l'a beaucoup secoué – he was shocked by
what the voters thought of him.

utilités (f);
jouer les utilités – to play second fiddle, be a minor player (the
image of the theatre and playing small parts; similarly, **jouer les
figurants**).

V

vacataire (m/f) – stand-in:
e.g., les professeurs ont travaillé dur, **les vacataires** aussi – all the
teachers have been working hard, the supply teachers included.

vague (f);
surfer sur la vague – to jump on the bandwagon:
e.g., les étudiants **surfent sur la vague** de ce nouveau mouvement
de protestation – students are jumping on the bandwagon of this
new protest movement.

valeur (f) **sûre**:
e.g., à cette époque votre père était une des **valeurs sûres** de notre
équipe – at that time your father was one of the top players in our
team;
leur champagne de maison est une **valeur sûre** – their house
champagne is very good, you won't be disappointed.

valse (f);
valse des étiquettes – round of price rises:
e.g., le ministre a refusé de commenter **la valse** actuelle **des
étiquettes** – the minister refused to comment on the present hike
in prices (**étiquette** = price tag);

valse-hésitation (f) – pussy-footing around:
e.g., après plusieurs mois de **valse-hésitation** – after several
months of pussy-footing around.

à vau-l'eau * – down the drain, going to the dogs:
e.g., tout va **à vau-l'eau** – everything is going downhill.

veilleuse (f);
mettre en veilleuse – to tone down, shelve:
e.g., Noël approche. Est-ce qu'ils vont peut-être **mettre** leurs
réclamations **en veilleuse**? – Christmas is getting near. Are they
perhaps going to shelve their claims?

vendu (m) * – traitor, double-dealer.

verrou (m):
e.g., les Américains espèrent faire sauter **les verrous** d'une paix
durable – the Americans hope to clear the way to a lasting peace.

vestiaire (m):
e.g., il a assisté à la réunion mais cette fois il a laissé ses préjugés **au**
vestiaire – he attended the meeting but this time he left his
prejudices behind.

vice (m);
pour vice de forme – on a technicality:
e.g., tous les deux ont été relaxés **pour vice de forme** – both of
them were released on a technicality.

vide (m);
vide juridique – legal loophole;
passage à vide – bad spell:
e.g., c'est vrai que notre équipe a eu un **passage à vide** – it's true
our team went through a lean spell.

vierge – blank;
une feuille de papier vierge – a blank sheet of paper

vilipender (literary) – to vilify.

viol (m) – rape;
viol collectif – gang rape.

violence (f);
la violence au volant – road rage.

violenter (quelqu'un) – to assault (sexually).

virage (m);
virage à 180 degrés – U-turn;
prendre le virage – to change course, go in a new direction:
e.g., ici tout change. On **a pris le virage** du 'nouveau' tourisme –
Here everything is changing. We have embraced the 'new' tourism.

visagiste (m/f) – beautician.

vis-à-vis (m);
sans vis-à-vis – with no buildings opposite, with a clear aspect to
the front (as in property advertisements).

viscérale – deep-rooted;
peur viscérale – deep-seated fear.

visé;
se sentir visé – to feel one is being got at, targeted.

visiter – to burgle:
e.g., hélas, notre résidence secondaire **a été visitée** pendant le week-
end – alas, our second home was broken into at the week-end.

vital;
le minimum vital – the bare minimum (to live on).

vitesse (f);
passer la vitesse supérieure – to change up a gear:
e.g., devant cette flambée de violence le gouvernement doit **passer la
vitesse supérieure** – faced with this flare-up of violence the
government must move up a gear.

voeux (m);
appeler quelque chose de tous ses voeux – to hope (with all one's heart) for something:
e.g., **j'appelle de tous mes voeux** un résultat favorable – I do hope the result will be favourable.

voiture (f);
voiture bélier – ram-raid car;
petite voiture – wheelchair.

voiturier (m) – person who will park your car:
e.g., encore un avantage, ce restaurant a un **voiturier** – another good point, this restaurant has valet parking.

voyagiste (m) – tour operator.

voyant (m) – warning light (also **témoin** (m) or **lampe** (f) **témoin**).

vue (f);
être placé en garde à vue – to be detained in custody (police).

W

warnings (m) – hazard lights:
e.g., oui, j'ai remarqué une voiture devant sa maison tous **warnings** allumés – yes, I noticed a car in front of her house with all its hazard lights on.

Z

zéro (m);
zéro calorie – calory free:
e.g., ça m'a coûté **zéro** euro – it didn't cost me a single euro;
ta soeur a fait **zéro** faute – your sister didn't make a single mistake.

zizanie (f);
semer la zizanie – to sow discord, cause unrest, stir things up.

zone (f);
zone de non-droit – no-go area:
e.g., le policier m'a dit carrément que là-bas c'était **la zone de non-droit** – the policeman told me straight out that over there was the no-go area;
zone d'ombre – grey area:
e.g., rien n'a été signé parce qu'il y a toujours des **zones d'ombre** – nothing has been signed because things are still not clear in places;
zone tampon – buffer zone.